Spelling in Use

Spelling in Use

Looking Closely at Spelling in Whole Language Classrooms

Lester L. Laminack
Western Carolina University

Katie Wood
Western Carolina University

with a Foreword by Sandra Wilde

Afterword by Lucy Calkins

National Council of Teachers of English
1111 W. Kenyon Road, Urbana, Illinois 61801-1096

Riverside Community College
Library
'98
MAR   4800 Magnolia Avenue
Riverside, California 92506

litor: Precision Graphic Services, Inc.

Production Editor: Marlo Welshons

Cover and Interior Design: Precision Graphic Services, Inc.

Compositor: Precision Graphic Services, Inc.

NCTE Stock Number: 46635-3050

It is the policy of NCTE in its journals and other publications to provide
a forum for the open discussion of ideas concerning the content and
the teaching of English and the language arts. Publicity accorded to any
particular point of view does not imply endorsement by the Executive
Committee, the Board of Directors, or the membership at large, except in
announcements of policy, where such endorsements is clearly specified.

Library of Congress Cataloging-in-Publication Data

Laminack, Lester L.,   1956–
    Spelling in use : looking closely at spelling in whole language
    classrooms / Lester L. Laminack, Katie Wood ; with a foreword by
    Sandra Wilde, afterword by Lucy Calkins.
        p.   cm.
    Includes bibliographical references and index.
    ISBN 0-8141-4663-5 (pbk.)
    1. English language—Orthography and spelling—Study and teaching
(Elementary)—United States.   2. Language experience approach in
education—United States.   I. Wood, Katie, 1964– . II. National
Council of Teachers of English.   III. Title.
LB1574.L36   1996
372.6'32—dc20   96-28685
                                                                        CIP

For all the children I put through spelling drills, exercises, and tests. I cringe when I remember those stars on the wall. Forgive me please, I didn't know better then.

And for Sandra Lawing, Dayle Keener, and Carol Sutton—insightful teachers, masterful kidwatchers, diligent advocates for children and teachers, valued colleagues, and treasured friends.

—LLL

For all the children who helped me see their brilliance, and for my parents, Paul and Christine Wood, who helped me to see mine, and for Jim Ray, who balanced everything out.

—KW

CONTENTS

FOREWORD

In the last twenty years, few areas of elementary school curriculum have changed more than spelling. Many of today's teachers grew up in the era of half an hour a day spent on spelling out of a textbook, with "creative writing" only on Friday afternoons, if at all. In the early 1980s, the writing revolution began, fomented by Donald Graves (1983), a revolution that would have been impossible in the primary grades and limited in upper grades without the invented spelling that we were beginning to learn about from Charles Read (1975) and others. But the spelling books were still firmly in place in most classrooms. Gradually, however, teachers began to question twenty words a week (and all the activities that went with them) that were unrelated to the writing process. They began to look at children who were actively thinking about how words are spelled and using a variety of useful strategies to come up with the spellings of words as they wrote. The teachers saw that children's spelling improved as they got older through seeing more words in print as part of extensive reading.

And these teachers' practices began to change. They stopped using the textbooks (and their districts stopped buying them). They placed spelling in the context of writing rather than in its own lengthy time slot every day. They paid attention to what children were doing and began teaching mini-lessons (with a whole class, with small groups, and with individuals) to prod students to the next step in their learning. Lester Laminack and Katie Wood's book both reflects and advances these changes in how we help children learn to spell.

Spelling, although a small piece of the writing process, is of great concern to teachers, parents, and the general public, so a great deal has been written about it. *Spelling in Use,* however, makes a number of unique contributions that make it especially valuable for classroom teachers. Those who write about spelling sometimes get caught up in the complex ins and outs of how the English spelling system works and how we might teach children all about it. Laminack and Wood, by contrast, stay focused on children, the writing process, and the everyday life of the classroom, so that common sense is this book's central quality (yet a common sense grounded in theoretical knowledge).

There are several highlights of their thinking that all teachers interested in helping children learn to spell better should keep in mind:

- Kidwatching is crucial and central. The best instruction grows out of paying close attention to what children are doing: looking at their spellings, noticing how they come up with spellings, and asking them about spelling.

- "Curriculum watching" is also crucial and central: noticing that words learned for a test don't always transfer to writing, but that learning a good spelling strategy has broad application.

- An informed, attentive teacher can create a powerful, effective curriculum in which spelling grows out of children's own explorations with spelling as they write.

This book has many highlights—voices of teachers describing how their spelling practices changed over time, varied ideas for working with parents, mini-lessons that illuminate but don't prescribe, close looks at children's writing accompanied by tools for assessing their growth as spellers—but I believe that teachers will prize it most for its combination of inspiration and practical sense, its deep knowledge that any curriculum works best when teachers pay attention to kids and then act on what they've learned from them.

—*Sandra Wilde*

ACKNOWLEDGMENTS

Many significant people helped us along the way as *Spelling In Use* came to be. First we would like to thank Dr. Mary Rose and the North Carolina Department of Public Instruction for recognizing the need for a book like this. *Spelling In Use* began as an NCDPI resource document for teachers in North Carolina.

We would like to thank the teachers in the original think tank who helped us develop ideas for the original NCDPI document. Sandra Lawing, Carol Sutton, Dayle Keener, and Norma Kimzey—your brilliant insights were (and continue to be) invaluable.

We also wish to thank all the teachers and children who invited us to work with them in their classrooms and provided us with the examples and writing samples.

Thanks to Shirley Bateman and Merry Woodard who support us daily with warm smiles, even when we don't deserve them.

Dawn Boyer. Thank you for believing in this project from the start and for all your advice along the way. You have been a valuable mentor and have become a treasured friend. Thanks also to Marlo Welshons for your continuous support and guidance.

INTRODUCTION

In whole language classrooms, instruction in spelling happens every day. This instruction is carefully and thoughtfully woven into and around the fabric of the work children do as writers throughout the day. Because this instruction looks so different from traditional spelling lessons, many adults have difficulty understanding how children are learning to spell in whole language classrooms and why approximations are valued and even celebrated when they are not "right." With new knowledge available about how children learn, all of us—teachers, parents, students, administrators—are rethinking, and rewriting a history of schooling that has sought to make all learning linear and sequential.

Through many encounters with children over several years, we have come to better understand how our instruction needs to follow children's real work as writers. Like many of our whole language colleagues, we are learning to get curriculum behind young writers so that it can propel them forward rather than block their paths. The journey has not always been easy or comfortable. We've shared many worries about whether children were "getting it" and whether we were "teaching it" enough. But time and again, children have shown us, as they have developed theories for how language works, that if we trust them as learners and support them through our teaching, they will learn more than we could ever plan for in a neat series of lessons planned apart from their lives as writers.

In the very heart of this book, we share the stories of teachers who've been on this journey of new understandings. They share a common vision for the writing curriculum in their classrooms. These teachers are not ignoring instruction in spelling. They are not oblivious to the need for writers to use conventional spelling in order to communicate powerfully through writing. Their focus is on the broader picture, the need to develop young writers who recognize the value of their own words and ideas. These teachers help their students see spelling as one of the many resources at their command to communicate with the world. In short, the focus of these teachers is on *spelling in use* rather than on spelling as an isolated fragment of the overall language arts curriculum.

The purpose of this book is to help those who interact regularly with young children understand how *learning to spell* is a part of the broader fabric of *learning to write* in whole language classrooms. This book is written primarily for classroom teachers and provides a practical look at the role of spelling in the overall language arts curriculum. The focus is on developing competent writers, with spelling as one aspect of that development. In this focus, spelling is seen not as a separate subject but as one facet of the writing curriculum.

Spelling in Use is organized into six chapters. In Chapter 1 we provide opportunities for you to explore how your own beliefs about language and literacy learning impact how you view your students' writing. We offer you the challenge to consider a more holistic point of view as you think about your own instruction.

Chapter 2 introduces three teachers who tell their personal stories of transition from a traditional approach to spelling instruction to incorporating the study of spelling in use in their whole language classrooms. Alongside each story is a running commentary that highlights the significant turning points in that teacher's professional development. This commentary reveals the guiding assumptions that influenced the curricular decisions each teacher made throughout her transition. This chapter closes with a summary that demonstrates how the changing views about spelling in these classrooms led to significant changes in the writing instruction. Eventually, all three teachers shared a common view of spelling in use as the best instructional approach for their writing workshops.

In Chapter 3 we provide suggestions that help you develop ways to systematically study and assess children's spelling in use, and then use these assessments to plan whole-class, small-group, and individually appropriate instruction. As you read this chapter, you will be encouraged to reconsider the traditional linear planning structure of curriculum–instruction–assessment. We suggest instead a "research, decide, teach" frame (Calkins 1994) in which assessment is thought of as research into what children are doing with spelling in their writing. Information generated from this assessment informs decisions about what to teach. We feel this kind of "assessment first" planning should be the norm for all writing curriculum development enacted by wise classroom teachers, not just in relation to spelling. Also embedded in this chapter are specific suggestions and vignettes from several classrooms that demonstrate the "research, decide, teach" model.

In Chapter 4, we present the "nuts and bolts" of spelling instruction in a whole language classroom. There is a sample schedule to demonstrate how spelling instruction might be organized and how time might be managed in the classroom. Several examples are provided, and classroom vignettes are used to illuminate strategies that are commonly used by teachers and students in whole language classrooms.

Chapter 5 provides practical help in communicating with parents about the teaching of spelling in use. The chapter covers four areas—workshops for parents, conferences with parents, individual letters to parents, and classroom newsletters. The chapter ends with a summary of the information we often share with parents in newsletter formats.

In the final chapter we respond to questions that teachers most often ask us about spelling instruction. We hesitate to call our responses "answers" in any singular sense. Instead, we demonstrate our thinking process as we suggest possibilities for finding the answers to these questions in the work children do as writers. We believe the questions cannot be considered apart from the young writers they address.

CHAPTER 1

Spelling—What's All the Fuss?

Spelling. What does that single word call to mind? Many of us think of spelling drills, writing each word five times, making a sentence with each word, and writing a paragraph with those sentences. Maybe you remember exercises *A, B, C, D,* a practice test on Wednesday, and the real test on Friday (unless you scored 100 percent on the practice test). You may recall spelling bees or that red *sp* mark inside the circle hovering above some word on your page.

Perhaps the lenses we use to view spelling are somewhat foggy or out of focus since we remember spelling drills, exercises, and tests, as do most adults. Our educational histories tremendously influence our adult perceptions of any situation that involves teaching and learning. Our histories also limit our own abilities to assess our personal learning. For example, if we consider ourselves decent spellers today, remembering those drills, exercises, and tests, we are very likely to attribute our knowledge to that style of instruction.

Consider the story below written by Carl, a second grader.

I have a bull dog. his name is
B. J. He is 6 years old
He has a black nose. He is
brown. Heis nose is flat
B. J. can pull me down hill.
B. J. can pull me up hill.
Me and B. J. are good friends.

What are your immediate reactions to this piece? What do you notice? Take a few moments and jot down your first thoughts in the space below.

FIRST REACTIONS:

Look again at Carl's piece and think about Carl's teacher. What would you say the teacher values in Carl's writing? Make a list of those things and indicate the evidence you find in Carl's piece:

Now consider this piece from seven-year-old Jason, also a second grader.

201 Steppe Street
Marion, NC 28752

Dear Ms. Goff,
   Thank you for playing the
piano for us. You played the
piano very good. I like music
class. Are we good singgers?
I will like to learn
how to play the piano.
Thank you for coming.
It was inbarusing to be
infrut of every body.
You are a very good
singger. Who tolt you to play
the piano? We like you.
Have you ever ben in
the hospitle? I love you.

                Love,
                Jason

What are your immediate reactions to this piece? What do you notice? Take a few moments and jot down your first reactions in the space below.

FIRST REACTIONS:

Now look again at Jason's piece and think about his teacher. What would you say Jason's teacher values in writing? Make a list of those things and indicate the evidence you find in Jason's piece.

As you read Carl's story you probably noticed the neatness, the conventional spellings, the spacing between words, and the use of punctuation. You may be thinking that this is a pretty good piece to get from a second-grade student. Look closely. Carl does have the conventions present in his writing, but at what cost? Whose voice is heard? What evidence do we have of his use of strategies for using language to express the experiences and ideas of his life? Look more closely. Read the piece aloud. Who do you hear in the piece? Is it the voice of a child? Or does it sound more like the pages of a primary reading program?

As you read Jason's story you probably noticed all the spelling "errors" immediately. That's what most adults notice. By looking into the familiar face of "error," however, we fail to see into the reflective eyes of approximation. Jason's piece has all the qualities we so cherish in Carl's story. Look closely and you will see the letter formation, the spacing between words, the use of capitalization and punctuation. It's all there and it is used conventionally.

One surface difference is the spelling. Look more closely. Did you notice that there were 82 words in Jason's story? Did you also notice that of the 82 words there were 53 different words? Did you notice that of the 53 different words 46 were spelled conventionally? That's right—there were only 7 constructed spellings! There are words very similar to those used by Carl, words such *are, is, the, I.* Now note the words for which Jason constructed a spelling, words such as *embarrassing, singer, taught, hospital.* When would most children meet these words in a traditional spelling program? How would they be encountered? Would they spill over into the writing of individual children? Why are they missing from Carl's writing?

You may find it interesting to know that Carl, whose piece was written in *April* of his second-grade year, had come to know reading through a basal reading program. He had come to know spelling through a spelling book with daily exercises and a weekly spelling list. Writing meant responding to a teacher-selected topic. Notice the similarity between Carl's written language and the "language" of many preprimer, primer, and early readers in a basal program.

Jason, whose piece was written in *September* of his second-grade year, had come to know reading through the words of the authors of children's literature. He had come to know spelling as an outgrowth of his writing, which was a way of finding information and sharing new insights and stories. Jason had power over words, a power that let him say what he wanted to just as he would in speech. In his letter to the music teacher, Jason focused on the message, telling what he felt was important and appropriate, using the words he chose to express those ideas. In his writing, Jason controls convention to say what he wants to say. Carl, on the other hand, limits his choice of words to those he can spell.

What is important about the stories of Carl and Jason? They help us gain new lenses for looking at children's work. Through these lenses we can see into the thoughts and language of the child's own life and begin to understand the world from the child's frame of reference. It enables us to stop staring into the familiar face of "error" and counting the "misspelled" words, "haphazardly used" punctuation marks, and "random" capital letters. It enables us, instead, to look deep into the reflective eyes of approximation and see the child's growing understanding of voice, audience, and the purposes for writing. We see the child's movement toward controlling convention rather than being controlled by it so that the child can *say what he wants to say as a writer*.

It is clear that writers are greatly influenced by what they read. Frank Smith (1988) put it this way: "We learn from the company we keep." This is evident in the work of Carl and Jason. Carl writes in the style of the basal readers he knows, and Jason finds his own voice to express his knowledge. What gives Jason the ability to put his voice on paper? Ralph Fletcher (1993) contends that writers need mentors and that the best mentors young writers can have are the authors of children's literature. Jason learns through reading that writing is an act of expressing what you know. He has had numerous demonstrations of how language works in reading, writing, listening, and speaking. He is comfortable with his knowledge, his language, and his ability to control written language well enough to communicate. Jason's level of comfort, his willingness to risk constructing a spelling for words he wants to write, comes from his assurance that his teacher will look past "error" and into the reflective eyes of approximation.

Spelling As an Extension of Children's Language Development

We have begun to see some changes in how schools approach the beginnings of reading with the attention given to emergent literacy. We now need to extend that acceptance of world knowledge, language competence, and concepts about print developed before schooling to our classroom practices with spelling.

We can't change our educational histories but we can begin to think about spelling as an extension of children's overall language development. Children do not learn oral language in one school year. Nor do they learn to listen and speak through a series of lessons arbitrarily ordered into an artificial hierarchy of scope and sequence. Instead, children become producers and consumers of oral language via their initiation into a community where significant persons around them produce and consume language. In such a setting, children are spoken to as if they understand, and they approximate the language used around them to communicate their own needs and thoughts. As individuals, children are treated as language users, fully competent members of the community. When children approximate language conventions in speech, adults tend to focus on communication. Adults restate a child's speech, ask questions for clarification, or respond normally as if to signal that the child's approximation is an appropriate and acceptable form. In each case the focus is on exchange of information, the construction of shared meanings. In short, the child is treated as a speaker. If this process begins at birth and forever continues in the development of oral language, should we not expect that it will be true of written language as well?

Because our educational histories limit our ability to view language learning as a natural process, we attempt to structure written language learning into discrete stages which can easily be organized into a series of lessons. We attempt to make school for our children what we remember it being for ourselves. It is important to note that, as *developmental stages* have been identified, there has been a tendency to organize curriculum and instruction around those stages and their characteristics. Such thinking about discrete stages tends to undermine the notion that there can indeed be continuous progress through normal development, and forces unrealistic expectations for some children.

There is also danger in trying to identify children's *levels* so as to instruct them through that level and on to the next. This line of thinking assumes that when one *new stage* begins, all previous ones have been forever completed, and those ahead are yet beyond reach and should become the next goal for instruction. This is not to say that there is no predictable pattern of development in moving from a child's first scribbles to conventional spelling in the process of becoming a competent writer. It is just that we cannot assume that spelling develops in a lock-step progression from one stage to the next. For example, functional writing (including constructed spellings) is a strategy that all writers use all of their lives. It is not a stage a writer outgrows with convention being the end goal. We do not, through a series of lessons, activities, or assignments, move a child along the continuum and through the stages to produce a writer who controls spelling by a given target date or grade in school.

If gaining control of conventional spelling does not proceed in a neat progression of stages, then how do competent writers learn to spell? Smith (1988) contends that "[t]here is only one way for anyone to become a speller and that is to find out and remember correct, i.e., conventional spellings." According to Smith, the only way it is possible for adults to write the scores of thousands of words they know is that they learned these spellings from *reading:* "The source of the information that makes us writers and speakers must lie in the language of other people, accessible only through reading and in listening to speech." Competent writers *did not* learn to spell the thousands of words they know *one at a time.* There were no single moments when competent writers suddenly came to own the spelling of each individual word they know, though most traditional spelling instruction is based on this false, one-word-at-a-time assumption.

At issue is the role of the adult in the natural development of the child's progression toward conventional spelling. We are less concerned with developing *competent spellers* than we are with developing *competent writers.* Therefore, it is more important to determine the strategies used by writers to produce spellings of words they need to communicate than to peg individuals as working at a particular level of development. Sandra Wilde (1989, 1992) contends that we should observe children's spelling strategies to gain insight into how spelling works in general and how individual children learn to control spelling as they grow into competent writers. To this end, Wilde (1989) states that as we look at children's spellings we must be guided by these four principles:

1. Spelling is evaluated on the basis of *natural writing* rather than tests.

2. Spelling is evaluated *analytically* rather than as merely right or wrong.

3. Spelling is looked at in terms of children's *strategies* rather than in isolation.

4. The teacher should evaluate spelling as an *informed professional* rather than as a mechanical test scorer.

This frame would have us focus on *how* children arrive at the spellings of words (conventional or not) rather than concentrating on whether the child arrived at the *correct* spelling. Among the primary goals of such a program would be to develop competent writers who use spelling to communicate—writers who learn to control conventions rather than being controlled by conventions. Toward this goal, Wilde (1989, 1992) identified five spelling strategies used by writers that must be valued by adults. From lower to higher level, these strategies are:

*   **Placeholder:** "I just wrote it that way."
*   **Human Resource:** "How do you spell *people*?"
*   **Textual Resource:** "I need the dictionary."
*   **Generation, Monitoring, and Revision:** "Say is *s-a-y*, huh?"
*   **Ownership:** "I know how to spell *rodeo*."

Higher-level strategies reflect an increasing reliance on one's own resources as a speller, yet may not produce more conventional spelling. Higher-level does not imply better.

Similarly, Bouffler (1984) has identified the following ten strategies:

1. **Spelling as it sounds**

    This refers to what is generally known as phonetic spelling and is based on the assumption of a direct

letter-sound relationship, e.g., "stashon" (*station*);
"sisers" (*scissors*).

2. Spelling as it sounds out

This strategy was identified as being used by children
but was not seen used by adults. It involves the exag-
geration of sound, so the phonetic features not normally represented are heard and represented, e.g.
"huw" (*who*); "hafh" (*half*).

3. Spelling as it articulates

This strategy makes use of the articulatory aspects of
sound, particularly place of articulation. Sounds are
represented on the basis of where they are made, e.g.,
"brif" (*brief*); "chridagen" (*tried again*).

4. Spelling as it means

This strategy represents semantic rather than phono-
logical units. It underlies much standard spelling, e.g.,
sign-signal; nation-nationality. Non-standard example:
"wasuponatim" (*Once upon a time*).

5. Spelling as it looks

All spelling involves this strategy to some extent. As its
name suggests, it uses graphic patterning, or visual memory, e.g., "oen" (*one*); "shcool" (*school*); "nigt" (*night*).

6. Spelling by analogy

This strategy is based on the principle that what has
been learned in one situation can be applied to another, e.g., "realistick" (*realistic*); "reskyou" (*rescue*).

7. Spelling by linguistic content

The spelling of a word may be affected by the linguis-
tic environment in which it occurs. It is not altogether

surprising to find *any* written immediately under the word *envelope* as *eny*.

8. Spelling by reference to authority

The authority may be other children, adults, or other writers (i.e., other written books or material). When other books, such as the dictionary, are used, we must employ all or some of the other strategies to find the word we are trying to write.

9. Opting for an alternative surface structure

If we do not know how to spell a word, we use a word we know we can spell.

10. Placing the onus on the reader

This strategy is used when text is handwritten. The writer makes the spelling indeterminate and leaves it to the reader to decide whether, for example, it is *ie* or *ei*.

Broadening the repertoires of spelling strategies employed by writers enables them to become more independent. Independence leads to more powerful writing. From this perspective, one role of the adult is to provide children with continuous demonstrations of various strategies for spelling. Consider the natural way adults tend to provide such support in the development of oral language. In this progression, adults provide demonstrations of language functions and forms, engage the child in conversations (uses of oral language), and respond to the child's approximations, giving the child further demonstrations regarding both function and form (Cambourne 1988; Cochrane, Cochrane, Scalena, and Buchanan 1984).

If we believe that spelling is part of writing, and that writing is part of the child's overall language development, we would approach spelling development in much the same way we would any facet of language development. Toward that goal we would encourage and support purposeful writing in the classroom. We would encourage children to attempt spellings independently before seeking assistance from an adult. The classroom would be filled with print resources and no strategy would be considered off-limits. And, as Wilde (1989) suggests, all strategies would be supported; no one strategy would be looked upon as being "better" than another. Strategies would be employed as they are needed. Children would write frequently for their own purposes using the words they select as those most appropriate for expressing their ideas.

To teach from this perspective, the teacher must know children, their histories, their personalities, and their development. It is only from this knowledge that we can teach into what the child knows and is trying to do. It becomes our responsibility as teachers to determine what the child *can* do and to use that information to make decisions about what to teach and how to teach it. Teaching then becomes a cycle of *research, decide, teach* (Calkins 1994). Our goal would be to help children grow into the hope we have for them as competent writers in their lives beyond our classrooms.

As professional educators, our assumptions about how children learn directly influence our classroom practices and our interactions with and expectations of the children we teach. We believe that children learn most naturally under the following conditions (Cambourne 1988, 33; Cambourne and Turbill 1991):

- **Immersion:** Learners need to be immersed in texts of all kinds.

- **Demonstration:** Learners need to receive many demonstrations of how texts are constructed and used.

- **Engagement:** Engagement occurs when learners are convinced that: (1) they are potential "doers" or "performers" of the demonstrations they are observing; (2) they will further the purposes of their lives by engaging with these observed demonstrations; (3) they can engage and try to emulate without fear of physical or psychological hurt if their attempts are not fully "correct."

- **Expectation:** Expectations of those to whom learners are bonded are powerful coercers of behavior. We achieve; we fail if we expect to fail; we are more likely to engage with demonstrations of those whom we regard as significant and who hold high expectations for us.

- **Responsibility:** Learners need to make their own decisions about when, how, and what "bits" to learn in any learning task. Learners who lose the ability to make decisions are "depowered."

- **Use:** Learners need time and opportunity to use, employ, and practice their developing control in functional, realistic, non-artificial ways.

- **Approximation:** Learners must be free to approximate the desired model—"mistakes" are essential for learning to occur.

- **Response:** Learners must receive "feedback" from exchanges with more knowledgeable "others." Response must be relevant, appropriate, timely, readily available, nonthreatening, with no strings attached.

What Does This Look Like in the Classroom?

When children are immersed in demonstrations of how texts are constructed and used, the classroom becomes a place where written language permeates the curriculum. Children are constantly using writing for various purposes such as making entries in writer's notebooks, jotting notes for their project files, documenting the growth of a plant on the window sill, or signing in each morning as they arrive. For example, consider the functions of language identified by Halliday (1975) and the classroom possibilities they imply.

Functions of Oral Language	Examples	Classroom Possibilities
INSTRUMENTAL LANGUAGE (communicating basic needs, gaining information, and solving problems)	"I'm thirsty; I need a drink of water." "I'm starting over because messed up." "Please give me some yellow paint."	sign-up sheet, catalog order, grocery list, wish list, planning list, business letter, memorandums, proposals
REGULATORY LANGUAGE (controlling behavior of others and the world around you)	"You put your truck over there and put a load on it and then bring it back to the warehouse."	directions, labels, rules for a game, signs, rules and regulations, procedures, advertisements
INTERACTIONAL LANGUAGE (language to establish and maintain relationships with others)	"Will you play a song with me?" "Let me help you find the book about Mars." "Joe, will you read with me, please?"	personal letters, jokes, and riddles, greeting cards, notes, invitations
PERSONAL LANGUAGE (language to develop and maintain one's own unique identity; say "who you are")	"We went to my cousin's house last night." "That was a scary story." "I can finally ride my bike!"	journals, diaries, autobiographies, eyewitness accounts, trip logs, editorials
INFORMATIVE LANGUAGE (language to represent the world to others; impart what one knows)	"Blue and yellow make green." "Not all newborn animals have their eyes closed." "Electricity made the bell ring." "The nails are heavier than the chips."	news articles, concept books, science logs, recipes, directions, posters, maps, booklets
HEURISTIC LANGUAGE (language to speculate and predict what will happen)	"Do you think the butterfly's wings are inside the caterpillar?" "I wonder if this will float." "Where does the sun go at night?"	question charts, hypotheses, reflective journals, exit slips
AESTHETIC LANGUAGE (language for its own sake, to express imagination, to play and have fun)	"I'm the mommy. Come home now." "Once upon a time . . ."	fiction tales, plays and skits, fairy tales, poetry

Language functions adapted from M. A. K. Halliday (1975). *Explorations in the functions of language*. London: Edward Arnold. Examples from North Carolina Department of Public Instruction (1989). *Grades 1 and 2 Assessment: Communication Skills*. Raleigh, North Carolina. Classroom possibilities from Norma A. Kimzey, Western Regional Technical Assistance Center–NCDPI, workshop handout.

In addition to engaging children in the many functional uses of language, it is important to bathe them in the language of authors they admire and introduce them to many new authors. Authors of children's literature (picture books, chapter books, poetry, nonfiction, etc.) become the mentors for student writers in the classroom. Language is one of several sign systems through which children construct new knowledge and express their understanding and questions. It is their questions that guide their inquiries and projects, it is their experiences in the world and with the language of authors that give rise to their topics, and it is the opportunity to use language in relevant ways that provides them with an awareness of and need for the conventions of written language. If we don't have children writing for their own purposes, we will not know what they can do or why they do it that way. We cannot assess the strategies used by children if all they know of writing is filling in the blanks, copying off the board, and mindlessly proceeding through the exercises in a workbook. Until children take risks with language to say the things they have a need to say, we will not have windows into their understanding of how language works.

CHAPTER 2

Teachers' Voices—Stories of Transition

In this chapter three teachers will tell their stories of making a transition from a very traditional, text-bound, linear approach of spelling instruction to teaching spelling in use. Each of these teachers brings two decades of classroom experience to this discussion. Dayle Keener teaches second grade in a small city school system. Carol Sutton, a former kindergarten teacher, has taught fifth grade for the last several years in a rural county school. Sandra Lawing is a Communication Skills Helping Teacher working with teachers throughout a school system. Her most recent classroom experience was as a K–1–2 multi-age teacher. We hope these teaching stories can serve as a mirror in which you see many of your own challenges reflected.

The overlaps in these stories are important because they uncover common shifts in thinking that occur as teachers make changes in the writing curriculum to address spelling in use. You will notice the following common themes in the stories. First, each teacher had to *learn more about writing* in order to think differently about spelling. Each teacher had to *learn to observe children* very closely to understand the changes that needed to be made in her spelling instruction. Each teacher acknowledged at some point that her *traditional spelling instruction was not helping* her students' spelling in use. Finally, the most important common theme in these stories is the fact that each teacher has many *lingering questions* about how to best help children grow in their knowledge of spelling in use.

In the following narratives, the teacher's story will be in the left column, accompanied by a running commentary in the right column. The commentary highlights the changes in each teacher's thinking that led to changes in classroom practice.

Dayle Keener's Story

I taught for several years treating spelling and written language as separate, isolated subjects. I valued the textbook because I needed it as my guide and decision maker. I valued only standard spelling. To me, a word was spelled either right or wrong. I typically introduced the words on Monday, assigned the daily exercises, and gave the test on Friday. When I think back, I don't remember children's spelling errors. However, I didn't provide many opportunities for any errors to occur. The children did language exercises from the textbook. They copied sentences, filled in blanks, and occasionally completed matching exercises. I avoided creative writing until absolutely necessary because I knew I couldn't write well. I felt so insecure. I thought, "how could I help children?"

The language curriculum was viewed as a fragmented and separated entity. The teacher viewed language as a subject to be taught, studied, and tested, rather than as a functional tool for communicating one's way through life.

Children's voices, student ownership, and spelling in use were not valued. Instead, the textbook, the manual, and standard spellings were valued.

The teacher's insecurity as a writer placed limitations on the opportunities she provided for children.

A turning point came when I participated in a writing project and entered graduate school. Some books I read first were: *Writing: Teachers and Children at Work* by Donald Graves, *Reading without Nonsense* by Frank Smith, and *What's Whole in Whole Language* by Ken Goodman. I began having the children write self-selected topics every day, keep writing folders of work in progress, share stories in teacher-supported helping circles, peer edit, and conclude with a final teacher-editing conference. The children published their favorite pieces of writing from those they had worked through the entire process. I noticed that when I valued the children's approximations in spelling, it freed them to take risks and to use more precise, interesting words. A stronger "voice" started to appear in their writing. The former skills I taught in isolation were all embedded in the children's writing. I conferenced individually and in small groups, and had mini-lessons as needed. I started to trust myself to make decisions about what the children needed to learn next. The children had a motivation and enthusiasm about their work that had not existed before I provided writing opportunities. Even though I accepted the children's individually constructed spellings, I continued to give spelling tests. I started noticing another pattern. The same children made the same grade from week to week. I could

Professional development (e.g., participation in a writing project, graduate school, professional reading) provided a needed knowledge base and a boost to self confidence that enables the teacher to work with the children in a writing community.

A slow transfer of ownership to children regarding topic, word choice, audience, and form. Writing is becoming something children do rather than something they simply know.

A focus on writing frees the children from bondage to words they know how to spell. They begin to see themselves as writers and focus more on choosing powerful words and thinking about what they want to say. In short, the teacher began to trust the children as writers.

The teacher began to carefully observe children as writers.

The children were growing in their developing sense of themselves as readers and writers.

predict the outcome of the test. The test took me thirty to forty minutes to get the children ready, give the test, collect the papers, and begin another use of this time. Most importantly, there was no transfer of learning to their writing. Over the past few years I have tried many methods and strategies. First, I tried content words in social studies and science. Then I focused on high-frequency words. This year I have been conscious about putting appropriate print in the classroom. In the writing center there is a word box with high-frequency words for each letter (i.e., words on a card, etc.). The materials that are stored in the classroom are labeled. As we have discussions (math, science, etc.), the students develop a list of words they need for that unit of study to help when they record their observations, thinking, and conclusions. At the first of the year, I chose four or five words in a spelling pattern (_ight). I did this simply as a management system that I could handle at the time. The children and I developed activities and games to practice the words. Now the children are using their pieces of writing or recordings in the learning log to select words that look close, but not quite right. The children are coming to me and saying, "I found 'my' word" (in books they were reading). One child corrected his words in a story he had written. Both of these experiences

The teacher began to recognize that the spelling tests were only measures of short-term memory with little or no carryover into the habits of children as writers.

There was a shift in the source of the words; however, the teacher still controlled the lists and owned the curriculum.

The teacher faced issues of time, management, routines, and trust.

A slow transition from a focus on words and a study of spelling for writing to *using spelling* in writing.

were student-initiated. Now the words belong to the children. I don't know if the children were ready (some still aren't) or if it was more what I should have done all year. I still have questions about how to manage all the children's growth and progress. And I still don't know if this is what I should be doing. I do know that the children's spelling approximations tell me what they know about print, letter sounds, chunks, and endings. What I do in the coming weeks will depend on new information I learn or what I learn from the children.

This questioning stance is at the heart of reflective practice. Reflective teachers are constantly examining their current practices and trusting children as their curricular informants.

Carol Sutton's Story

"I went to the mall yesturday." How well I remember seeing a sentence like that as I would read an entry in a student's journal. I also remember the overwhelming sense of frustration that would come over me as I would notice that the misspelled word, "yesturday," had been in the list of words that had been in our spelling textbook the previous week. What else could I do? Weekly, each student had to write every word five times and even had to use the word in a sentence. In addition, the word had to be looked up in the dictionary and written with the definition beside it. I rarely skipped any of the activities in

Early in the teacher's transition there was a sense of frustration with the lack of carryover.

The program was sequenced, highly organized, and very easy to follow. It provided the teacher with a sense of security and removed the need for her to make professional decisions based on specific knowledge of the children in her charge.

the spelling book. *A* on Monday, *B* on Tuesday, and *C* on Wednesday were regular assignments each week. We even played games and had spelling bees with the words! I felt that I was teaching spelling, but I continued to be aware that students who could make a perfect score on Friday's test couldn't spell the same words the next time they needed to write them. Why were my students not better spellers? What could I do differently?

The focus was clearly on individual words, not on the building of ideas through writing.

As I reflect on the communication skills program several years ago in my fifth grade classroom, I can remember the activities of a typical day. In addition to spelling, the schedule always included a reading lesson from a basal text. There were very few "real" books in our room, and most students never read anything but the reading assignment. Lessons from our English textbooks addressed language grammar and mechanics skills. Workbooks and worksheets which accompanied each of our books were used on a regular basis. Occasionally my students wrote in journals, but most "creative" writing occurred only when I assigned the students a topic, explained how much had to be written, and announced the due date. To be honest, my job was not personally challenging, and many times it was actually boring. Was it any wonder that my students were not enthusiastic about reading and writing?

The focus of the curriculum *was the textbooks,* not the students' growth as readers and writers. There were no obvious connections between reading, writing, and spelling. There were separate textbooks for each, and each was taught as a specific and separate subject.

During this time, I began hearing about something referred to as writing process. My initial reaction was that there was not enough time in the day to cover all of the material, and I certainly could not add anything else! The very idea that I could work with individual students was preposterous!

Fortunately, my sense of frustration with my current teaching strategies led me to continue listening to ideas about using a process approach to writing instruction. I signed up for an in-service and began by simply involving my students in finding their own topics. While students were busy working in their spelling and English books (I was not ready to give them up!), I would meet with a student to discuss his or her writing, mainly focusing on the mechanics of the piece.

As I began allowing students to choose topics for writing stories and reports, I noticed that they had more interest in their work. As a result, most students began writing more, and I began to be aware that spelling instruction could take place as I helped a student to edit. It was not difficult to detect when a student was experiencing difficulty with a particular spelling pattern (doubling consonants, for example) and make the student aware of it. Since the pieces of writing were important to the students, they were more interested in what I was saying

Frustration was growing with the current practices. Such frustration can lead to fear of change that can either immobilize or become the catalyst that pushes a teacher forward. In this case it helped the teacher seek new ideas and professional development opportunities.

The focus is shifting from spelling as content to writing as a process. With a new investment in their writing, both the students and the teacher began to see a better reason to study the conventions of language (e.g., spelling, punctuation, etc.).

The teacher sees that she can plan for spelling instruction from what she observes in her students' writing. This marks the beginning of a move away from textbook-driven instruction.

about their spelling. I was able to make connections that were impossible when teaching a list of words from a spelling textbook that had no personal meaning to the writer.

I was still concerned, however, that I was leaving too much to chance. I felt that I could now give up my spelling textbook, but not without replacing it with a list of words that I would teach to the students each week. Words from a reading story or a science unit were assigned each week, and students were to memorize them for the test on Friday. I guess I thought that students would find the task easier since the words I chose were from academic areas which were already being addressed. What I thought would happen did not, and again I felt a great deal of frustration.

At this time in my transition, I had so many questions which continued to grow every day. As a result, I began reading books and articles and attending conferences and in-services that addressed writing. It seemed to me that the only lasting spelling instruction that was taking place in my classroom was when it came from an individual's writing. Nothing I heard or read told me every step to take. Every word that I needed to say was not in bold-faced type. I learned, however, about ways other teachers implemented the process of writing in their classrooms, and I got enough suggestions so that I

There was a change in the source of the words selected for spelling, making them more connected to the active curriculum. However, the teacher still controlled the words available to the children. There was no ownership for the child as the teacher moved from spelling textbooks to content area vocabulary. Although the teacher recognized the need for change, the focus was still on words.

The teacher was slowly coming to understand that she would have to be the instructional decision maker if she was to focus on spelling in use. Toward that end, she realized the need to shift the focus from studying words for spelling to writing.

could begin trying some new strategies. I liked the challenge of making decisions concerning what a student knew and what he or she was ready to learn next. The main thing that I learned was that students learn how to spell as they read and write, not as they commit a list of words to their short-term memory. My challenge was to create an environment in my classroom so that students would want to read and write!

The teacher has a new theory base for her belief system. This will come to impact her future instructional decisions.

My classroom today is very different. As I see the connections between reading and writing and have learned to trust myself and my students more, I have gradually given up the basal reading text and have developed a classroom library. Students are learning to be better readers and writers (and, yes, spellers) as they are allowed to choose what they want to read from books that were written by quality children's authors. Opportunities for writing occur throughout the day as my students respond to the literature, write letters to pen pals, and keep logs in all of the other content areas. They also are continually drafting, revising, editing, and publishing pieces of writing.

The teacher provided many opportunities for reading and writing so that spelling growth could occur. The spelling curriculum is now generated by the work of young readers and writers; the teacher no longer abdicates her professional judgment to the distant authors of some spelling textbook.

As students are reading and writing, I am conferencing with individuals and small groups. I am able to make suggestions concerning content, and when the student is ready to edit, I can teach all of the spelling and language skills that are appropriate for this

The teacher is in transition toward a more comprehensive literacy program. There is emphasis on creating a balanced writing program to develop spellers.

child. As I mentioned earlier, the instruction is now connected to something that is personal and meaningful to each child, instead of being a set skills taught in isolation.

Large-group instruction in spelling still occurs. I teach mini-lessons to call attention to a pattern that is giving difficulty to a large number of students. I also use this time to discuss various spelling strategies so that students will have some choices of what to do when they don't know how to spell a word. Students also focus on a few words each week as they choose some words they know are giving them difficulty in their own writing. Personal dictionaries kept by each student are also helpful.

In addition, I think it's important that I continually convey to my students the importance of conventional spelling any time they are writing for another person to read. My expectations are clear as students write pieces such as pen pal letters and thank-you notes and prepare them for publication. One way that I assess grades for the report card is how well various pieces are edited for spelling.

The story of my transition does not end here. It will be a continual process of change and growth as I learn more about the connection between writing and spelling. I am always questioning my current methods and searching for more efficient ones, but I believe that deliberate and systematic teaching and

There is a focus on strategies instead of words. The teacher provides mini-lessons to demonstrate the strategies writers use to spell words they do not yet "own."

The teacher now helps the children focus on their writing audience rather than viewing writing as simply a display of their control of convention.

This questioning stance is at the heart of reflective practice. Wise teachers are constantly examining their current practices and using children as their curricular informants.

testing of a list of spelling words is ineffective. As in the past, my transition will continue to be slow but also exciting. Also, I will not discard current techniques for spelling instruction until I understand the rationale for a new practice and can explain it to administrators and parents. My goal is to be continually moving toward a total communication program where spelling is never viewed as an isolated subject and where children view themselves first as readers and writers and then as capable spellers.

The teacher's theory base for her belief system is clearly valued.

Sandra Lawing's Story

Anthony was my best spelling teacher. In twenty years of teaching, with some of the best spelling "teachers" I could have—Graves, Calkins, Wilde, peers, and mentors—Anthony was the teacher who made the most significant difference in my knowledge of spelling development. He was a second grader in my class the second year of my trying the writer's workshop. I knew very little about writing or spelling or how children learned either one. Anthony trusted me anyway.

He was a small, beautiful boy with black hair and big, almost black, eyes.

He was still trying to make sense of print—with writing, especially. He was very tentative and didn't take risks easily. The words in his meager attempts at stories would often begin with the appropriate letter and just as often end with *ony*. It took me a little while to realize that when he had no idea of the conventional spelling, he used the few safe letters he already knew—those in his name!

I began to watch more closely Anthony's progress as a speller and writer. With many spelling support systems in place—meaningful print, lots of books and reading, strategy lessons, etc.—Anthony gradually began to use some appropriate ending letters. His progress was beginning to show on spelling tests as well. Unfortunately, there was no grading on progress—only on right or wrong. His test grade was always failing—which only undermined any risk taking that was necessary for continued confidence and growth. I was beginning to understand that the spelling test was neither a fair nor accurate record of children's progress as spellers; it was serving no purpose to Anthony as a writer or to me as a teacher. I shudder to think of the emotional trauma I was causing Anthony each week at test time. I knew it was time to tackle the issue of using the spelling test as an indicator of spelling progress. It was time to value spelling for its use—within the context of each

The teacher was an observer, a kidwatcher who viewed the children in her charge as curricular informants.

The teacher is building a theory of the child that will help her make appropriate instructional decisions.

As the teacher came to recognize that the spelling tests were neither fair nor accurate, her knowledge of writing was also growing. It was at this point that she began to value spelling in the context of writing.

child's writing. I had already made the step out of a spelling text and had been creating a class list of words from the children's writing. I was confident enough now to give up the spelling test altogether. Could I find enough support from the administrators and parents?

I began reading a lot about writing and spelling so that I could present my "case" to the principal. I saved samples of children's writing to show progress over time. I talked with peers, mentors, and some parents. When I felt I was ready to present my case and defend my beliefs, I went to the principal. With her support, we discussed a campaign to help the parents better understand our view of spelling and writing. We wanted them to know that we still valued spelling but only within the context of real writing. We agreed that on the report card we would not eliminate the word "spelling" but would include it with the writing grade. I wrote a letter to the parents offering my time for conferences. I made copies of articles to share with them. I put together simple writing portfolios showing each child's progress in spelling and writing. I was ready.

It was a successful campaign. Most parents remembered their experiences with spelling tests. Many felt they were not good spellers despite years of having used spelling textbooks. For the most part, as long as parents could be assured that their children were making

The transition becomes an issue of developing a theory base. This comes about through reading, attending conferences and workshops, and participating in ongoing conversations with peers and mentors. In addition, the teacher was constantly reflecting on her practice in the classroom.

Note that most adults know about school through their own histories as students. For many (teachers and parents), this becomes a barrier in even considering any innovative practice.

progress, they supported our decision. They felt the experiences their children were having with writing were much more comprehensive, beneficial, and a better use of time than the spelling activities they had known as children. When parents reviewed published books and written stories side by side with a list of isolated words, they felt the stories and books gave everyone a better picture of what spelling was for than the test did. And the stories gave everyone something far more valuable to save, share, and celebrate. Of course, there were some parents who continued to have concerns and who still, after eight years, feel their children are poor spellers because they didn't have spelling tests in second grade!

The focus had become developing the children as writers.

Removing the fear of the test each week gave Anthony added confidence with his writing. Although he was still very tentative as a writer, he began taking more risks and using more strategies with his spelling—classmates, books, placeholders. It was a relief and a boost to his writing to know that he could go back later and "fix it up"—an option he didn't have on the spelling test. I'm sure that by placing so much value on the test, I was giving Anthony, a child who had limited knowledge of print, the idea that conventional spelling was a must at all times. Yes, I'm sure Anthony's spelling grade would have probably improved with the tests.

One year of innovative practice can no more be blamed for a child's failure eight years later than it can be credited for another's success.

By demonstrating that she valued writing, the teacher enabled Anthony to focus on what he had to say. Spelling now had a function—to permit him to communicate to an audience beyond himself. His focus could be on learning to control conventions to accomplish his own goals.

The teacher recognized that shifting the emphasis from words to writing was essential to facilitating the development of readers and writers.

However, those tests were hiding and hindering his knowledge of writing and crippling him as a writer. I was unknowingly putting obstacles in Anthony's path to learn instead of providing the scaffolding and support he needed.

Anthony trusted me to know what was best for him. I could have very easily let him and many others down. I'm glad Anthony was my teacher—but not because of what he taught me about spelling. Because Anthony taught me to put the child—not the curriculum, textbook, or grade—first, I learned to involve, teach, trust, and value the *child*.

As they make instructional decisions, teachers must be learning advocates for their students, teaching into their strengths instead of exposing their weaknesses.

My experiences with Anthony taught me to keep a proper perspective and a watchful eye on my students. Somehow my impact on Anthony's progress as a speller pales in comparison to the significant impact he had on my progress as a teacher and a learner.

The teacher's transition involved her becoming a teacher-researcher. She was a colearner in a community of scholarship who learned to "*research, decide , and teach.*"

Parallel Changes in Spelling and Writing

One of the most significant insights for these three teachers as they made changes in their spelling instruction was recognizing the need to make major changes in their writing instruction. Each teacher arrived at a point where "spelling" lost its identify as a distinct curricular area and became an integral part of the overall literacy instruction through the writing workshop. The chart that follows highlights the parallel changes the teacher made in the writing and spelling curriculums and instruction.

Spelling	Writing
Use spelling textbook, exercises A,B,C, D, word list; write each word five times, cover and write, look up words in the dictionary and write definitions, use each word in a sentence, combine the sentences into a paragraph, play spelling games (e.g., base-ball) with the words; do a practice test on Wednesday and final test on Friday.	Using worksheets/English book, exercises, copying from charts/board with emphasis on handwriting, grammar, copying basic sentence structures, copying to correct capitalization, punctuation.
Keep the spelling textbook, drop the exercises (A,B,C,D), and continue with the practices described above.	No change.
Let go of the spelling textbook; keep a list of words selected by the teacher, usually taken from the content areas (math, science, social studies, health, and occasionally from stories from reading); doing some activities or games, writing words five times each, looking up definitions, using the words in sentences; doing a practice test on Wednesday, and final test on Friday (teacher believes this is integrating spelling in the curriculum).	Keeping the English textbook/worksheets; children are writing in response to teacher-selected topics (creative writing once a week), length determined by the teacher.
The teacher still is selecting a few words from the content areas and layering in high-frequency words, emphasizing patterns/rules selected by the teacher; continuing the practice test on Wednesday and final test on Friday; may be using activities such as word walls or making words; letting go of writing each word five times, writing definitions, and writing sentences.	Rigid, teacher-controlled attempt to implement writing process (Monday—prewrite, Tuesday—draft, Wednesday—revise, Thursday—edit, Friday—publish): Teacher assigns some topics and occasionally allows choice from a set of topics. Teacher occasionally allows children to choose topics for "creative writing."

Spelling	Writing
Moving away from selecting words from the content areas, the teacher now selects some words and the class adds some words for the list; teacher drops the practice test on Wednesday, but continues the final test on Friday.	The teacher is beginning to trust the children more as writers, allowing more choice over topic and form; more writing is occurring; the teacher is providing more opportunities for writing.
The teacher selects some words for the whole class and each child selects some for an individual list.	Children are choosing topics for writing; the teacher demonstrates more trust in the children as writers and continues a focus on process with guidelines that permit flexibility to allow the children to move through a piece of writing at their own pace. The class is moving toward the writing workshop.
Children are selecting words for personal lists and are testing with a partner or self-testing; the teacher is focusing on the child as a writer with emphasis on his or her control over language; spelling is seen as a part of the child's overall language competence.	The teacher is learning more about management and organization of the writing workshop.
There is more emphasis on writing; children identify words from their own writing to address in their spelling study; lists are now made with a purpose of discussion and further study rather than for testing. There is an emphasis on teaching and learning strategies for spelling; children are correcting words in their writing by using sources in the room.	The teacher is shifting responsibility for improvement of writing to the child. Writers are now in charge of their own work.

Spelling	Writing
The teacher is teaching strategies, offering mini-lessons through a balanced writing program. Spelling is seen as a service to writers: writers strive to control conventional spellings rather than being controlled by them. Children are responsible for their spelling, going through written pieces and editing with a partner before publishing to bring words for the group discussion on strategies and things to know about spelling. There is an emphasis on spelling in use; the teacher is looking at progress evident in the children's writing samples; attention is given to audience, purpose, and form; the teacher is conferencing with small groups and individuals.	Children are working on their writing every day; they talk about their writing with others (peers and teacher); children make most of the decisions about their writing (topics, genres, audiences, revisions—how and when, publishing—when). The teacher decides which mini-lessons are appropriate for which children and when; the teacher confers every day to make curricular decisions for the class and for individual children; the teacher is guided by conferences with children, professional resources, and his/her vision for the children as writers; the teacher lets children make decisions about their writing and he/she makes decisions about teaching.
	At this point, students are reading daily from a variety of genres for various purposes—author studies, topic studies, personal inquiries, literature studies.

The Star

Tonight,
I'll wait until
The sun has finished
His homework
And gone to bed.
Then I'll tiptoe outside
And climb
My apple tree.

From the highest branch
I will search the night
For my special star.

I will pluck
It from the sky
As if it were an apple
On my tree.

Then I'll put it in my pocket,
And keep my secret
Hidden
Until our spelling test.

Tomorrow,
When my teacher
Gives out the stars
To all the good spellers,
I won't be sad,
Because I'll have
One, too.

—Kalli Dakos

CHAPTER 3

Assessment First: Planning for a Writing Curriculum That Deals Responsibly with Spelling

The key to dealing responsibly with spelling in any successful writing program is *assessment of spelling in use*. Teachers must have ways to systematically study and assess children's spelling in use and then use these assessments to plan both whole-class and individually appropriate instruction. Curriculum and instruction in spelling must be connected to children's writing if it is to be effective. We do make a distinction here between *assessment* and *evaluation*. Assessment of spelling in use is an attempt to understand how young writers are dealing with both familiar and unfamiliar spellings they encounter in their personal writing so that instruction can improve. Evaluation, on the other hand, is an attempt to value or devalue children's spelling use and does not, we have found, lead to better instructional decisions. Evaluation may have a place alongside assessment, but it certainly has no merit of its own.

Planning for this kind of writer-centered curriculum in spelling takes place in a frame that always begins with *assessment research,* moves to *curricular decisions,* and then to *instructional interactions.* This of course rearranges the traditional linear planning structure of curriculum first (What should I teach?), instruction second (How will I teach it?), and assessment last (Did they get it?). Instead, in this "research, decide, teach" frame (Calkins 1994), assessment comes first and is not about "Did they get it?" but "How are they using it?" Assessment is thought of as research into what children are doing with spelling in their writing. We ask questions such as, "What strategies are they using? What risks are they taking? How is reading influencing spelling in their writing?"

Questions such as these give much-needed insight to teachers as they make curricular decisions that are appropriate for both individual children and the larger community of writers in the classroom. These decisions are embedded in the work of young writers, and they are tied directly to a vision teachers hold for their students as competent writers and for the place of spelling control in that vision. For example:

- Sharisse's fourth-grade teacher observes and notes that Sharisse looks up each unfamiliar spelling she's using as she is drafting. She uses this observation to plan a lesson on placeholder spelling.

- Marcus's first-grade teacher studies his papers and sees the wide range of "risky" words he uses to say what he wants to say in his writing—words like "exactly" and "pretend" and "carefully." She plans a mini-lesson in which Marcus will share with other students how he generates the spelling of any word he wants to use.

Instructional interactions that teach writers about spelling occur in several formats, including one-to-one conferences, small groups, and whole-class gatherings. Instructional interactions also take a variety of forms ranging from strategy sharing to focused discussions and inquiries. For example:

- After one writer struggles with the spelling of "boating" (he wants to double the *t*) as he writes about a boating accident, Roberto and his third-grade students become interested in the doubling of final consonants when suffixes are added. They make a chart in the room where students write any "doubling the consonant" words they find as they read and write over several days. Studying the patterns of the words they've collected, the students generate "rules" that will help them in most cases with this spelling pattern.

- A second-grade teacher has noticed a group of students who seem to rely only on "sounding out" as a generating strategy. She gathers them at a table and explains to them that words are like "people's faces" and that writers try to remember what words look like as they write—just like the faces of people they know. She tells the students that if they want to use a word they've only heard, but have never seen "in person" as they are reading, they may then rely on "sounding out" as a strategy.

We feel this kind of "assessment first" planning should be the norm for all writing curriculum development enacted by wise classroom teachers, not just in relation to spelling. Embedding our curricular decisions in children's writing requires that we think of assessment as research into what our students are doing and move this research to the forefront of our planning. The following sections are organized in this "research, decide, teach" frame. Each section includes practical classroom possibilities to help teachers begin to work within this nontraditional planning frame.

Research

Observing and Researching

To begin an assessment program of research which informs
spelling curriculum, teachers must become habitual kidwatchers and observe students as they write. As teachers observe
children at work on writing, they may ask questions to help
understand what they see writers doing, they may takes notes
that will help them plan later instruction, and/or they may
help a student with a spelling "bug" as they see it occurring.
These teachers are trying to capture spelling in use as they
systematically watch their students write in order to plan instruction from this. All of the examples in this book show
teachers making instructional decisions based on what they
see their students doing as writers. The curriculum grows
from the work of real writers. It is extremely important here to
point out that we focus on spelling decisions in this book because that is our topic. These teachers, however, are making
all kinds of curricular decisions—everything to do with their
writing curriculum—as they watch children write and interact
in the writing workshop. They are planning for and teaching
on-the-spot lessons on revision, writing structures, genre information, voice, and so on. These teachers believe that children hold the clues to a writing curriculum that will make
sense in the room.

Observing Young Writers

With less experience to support them, young writers must
focus more deliberately on generating spellings as they
write. By observing young writers in action, wise teachers
can often determine which strategies the children are using
to generate spellings in their writing. The following are some

observational guidelines that will help teachers as they
think about the strategies children are using.

- *Does the child's mouth move constantly as he or she
  writes?* If so, the child is probably relying primarily on
  "sounding out" to spell. When a child begins to move
  his or her mouth only on more challenging words, this
  is a sign of growth because the child is calling up this resource only when others prove insufficient.

- *How quickly is the child writing?* If the writing is extremely slow and labored, the child may be overly conscious about generating spellings or may not have
  enough useful strategies to help with generations.
  Either difficulty can inhibit growth as a writer. If the
  child is writing very quickly, she may not be drawing
  heavily enough from the supports that are there to help
  her. What we want is a steady, thoughtful pace to a
  young child's writing.

- *Listen to the child's interactions as he writes.* Does he use
  others as resources? Does he see himself as a resource
  for others? Again, look for a balance in the conversations about spelling. You want children to see each
  other as resources for lots of help as writers, not just
  spelling help. But if a child seems overly focused on getting spelling help from others and is not taking enough
  risks on his own, you may need to reinforce the other
  strategies.

- *Follow the line of the child's vision as she writes.* Do you
  notice that the environmental print in the room is directly
  influencing the child as she writes? If so, does it seem to
  be a positive influence (helping occasionally) or a nega-
  tive one (closing down risk taking)? Sometimes, print that
  is meant to help a child actually hinders her growth. For
  example, a box or a dictionary of "words I want to know
  how to spell" may become the only words the child will
  use as she writes. If so, this list may need to go.

Some Questions to Ask Writers About Spelling

Young writers in classrooms where assessment precedes curriculum are accustomed to their teachers asking them questions of process. Writers who are frequently asked process
questions must think about the ways in which they are working, and this helps them access their own strategies. Like observations, the information these questions yield helps
teachers make curricular decisions. The following questions
are examples of strategy questions.

- How do you think of the ways to write words?

- What do you think about when you come to a word that
  is difficult for you to spell?

- Do you notice spellings as you read?

- What are some of the words that are very easy for you
  to spell?

- Do you ever change a word if the spelling doesn't look
  right to you?

- Are there words you can spell without even thinking
  about them?

- Do you think that spelling is easy or hard? Why? (Answers often offer many insights.)

Researching Pieces of Children's Writing

Artifacts such as writing samples should be periodically
copied and saved with accompanying observations about the
child's spelling in use. These documents and teachers' observational notes may be kept in folders for individual students
and should be used in place of grades to communicate to children and parents about writing growth and the role of spelling

in that growth. Again, we will make the point that we highlight spelling because it is the purpose of this book to do so, but we feel these assessment practices are sound ones for all dimensions of children's work as writers.

When wise teachers look at children's writing samples, they frame their looking as research and, with regard to spelling, are curious about matters such as generating and placeholding strategies, risk taking (spelling a difficult word), and ownership (words that have become automatic). Two assessment tools, one a question and one a formula, are useful for looking at children's writing samples and understanding the growth of children as writers.

A Question: "Generating Spellings." When you see nonconventional spellings, make sure your question is, "What smart thing has this child done to generate this spelling?" Children spell in ways that make sense to them. The teacher's role is to identify this making sense and, based on it, either confirm smart strategies and/or show children how to do something they are not yet doing as writers. For example, when seven-year-old Catherine writes "Lejens in the Pole" (Legends in the Pool) as the title of her new scary story, her teacher realizes that Catherine has spelled *pool* based on what she knows about another word pattern that sounded similar and was familiar to her—*role, pole, hole.* Her teacher confirms that this is a smart strategy to use when Catherine is unsure of a word, and she goes on to show Catherine how *pool* is, in fact, like a number of other words she knows—*tool, fool, cool,* and, of course, *school.*

A Formula: "Index of Control." An index of control gives a researching teacher a numerical measure of a writer's control over the spellings the writer chooses to use in his or her writing when given the opportunity to write in his or her own voice. The index of control is a helpful way to see whether a writer is controlling convention or is being controlled by it. Because the index of control generates numerical data on a writer, there is a danger that this data could be misused to give children grades. We feel strongly that this research tool should not be used in this way. If writers learn that there are penalties tied to their risk taking, they undoubtedly will take the safest course as writers and use only those words whose spellings they own.

You will find that using the index of control is a time-consuming process, but the data it provides (as later samples show) is invaluable. Because of the time investment, however, we recommend that an index of control be done periodically throughout the year, more often with writers who are struggling or who present you with teaching anomalies where spelling is concerned. Here are the six steps for finding an index of control on a child's writing sample:

1. Collect samples of the student's writing over a specified period of time.

2. Count the number of words in each sample.

3. Count the number of different words in each sample. For example, if the word *work* appears in a piece eight times, it will be counted only once.

4. Of the total number of different words, count the number of those spelled conventionally (as in the dictionary).

5. Of the total number of different words, count the number of those words for which the writer constructed a spelling.

6. Divide the number of words spelled conventionally (Step 4) by the total number of different words (Step 3) to determine the index of control.

A. _____ = # of total words

B. _____ = # of different words

C. _____ = # of those spelled conventionally

D. _____ = # of constructed spellings

Index of Control = C divided by B

Index of Control = _____

Keeping Track of Individual Spelling Growth. You may find it helpful to develop a record sheet for documenting growth in spelling control over time. A record sheet might include the following useful information about writing samples throughout the year:

1. growth in the total number of words used in a writing sample

2. growth in the number of different words used in the sample as an indication of increased written verbal fluency

3. growth in the writer's index of control

4. the writer's continuing focus on communication of meaning and sensitivity to word choices

Over time, you may notice that a student shows increases in the total number of words and the number of different words, and maintains or increases the "index of control." In such a case, you would note that the student shows development as a speller in that the total number of words spelled conventionally is increasing. This pattern indicates that the writer is concerned with the expression of ideas and is willing to continue taking risks with unknown spellings while gaining control over an increasing number of words used frequently in writing.

If you should notice that a student's writing shows no steady increase in either the total number of words or in the number of different words paired with an increasing index of control, your conclusions should be quite different. This scenario could indicate that the writer has shifted the emphasis from expression of ideas and word choice to "using words I can spell." This focus may result in "better" spelling in the individual's written products, but it may also result in loss of the writer's voice, restricted word choices, and less elaboration or detail. If this happens, you lose powerful opportunities to note the writer's strategies, strengths, and areas of need as a child deals with spelling in use.

You may find it helpful to list constructed spellings. Organize them into categories on the basis of similarities in spelling patterns (e.g., *-ake, -ight* patterns or words where the *f* sound is spelled *ph,* etc.). This clustering will be helpful in determining which patterns are most unfamiliar to the writer and where instruction will be most immediately relevant.

As an example, try using this method on the following writing sample. Angie, the writer, is a seven-year-old in a small rural school where she is in a K–1–2 multi-age classroom. When reading over this piece, what do you notice immediately?

What is a Nurse
She is someone that
helps people. Nurses Help
Doctors and, farmases.
Nurses get sick too.
When people get sick
Nurses help them. They
work in hospils and
Nurseing homes and Doctor's
offics. We apuashate
Nurses.
The End

Many adults immediately focus on the "errors" that are obvious in the piece. For example, they tend to notice the misplaced capital letters and misspelled words. We would like you to take a moment to look closely at Angie's writing sample and recognize the knowledge this young writer brings to the piece.

Make a list of the words Angie uses in her piece. As you complete the list, note the variety of words used and the spellings. We find it helpful to write the piece in columns, separating conventional spellings from constructed spellings, and placing a tally mark (/) next to the word each time it is repeated. (We also provide the conventional spelling for each constructed spelling.)

Conventional Spellings		Constructed Spellings
What	is /	farmases (*pharmacists*)
a	Nurse	hospils (*hospitals*)
She	someone	Nurseing (*nursing*)
that	helps	offics (*offices*)
people /	Nurses ///	apuashate (*appreciate*)
Help, help /	Doctors	
and //	get /	
sick /	too	
when	them	
they	work	
in	homes	
Doctor's	We	
The	End	

Using the Index of Control formula for Angie's piece, notice the following:

A. 41 = # of total words

B. 31 = # of different words

C. 26 = # of different words spelled conventionally

D. 5 = # of different words with constructed spellings

26 divided by 31 = .8387 × 100% = 83.8%

Index of Control = 84%

By using this information, you may have a different view of the child as a writer. For example, as you read Angie's writing, did it occur to you that she was controlling the spellings for more than 80 percent of the words she wanted to use? Did you focus on all that Angie could do or was your initial assessment based on collecting evidence regarding her needs? Did you focus on her strengths or her weaknesses? Notice the knowledge she demonstrates in the piece. Notice the word choices (*pharma-cists, nursing homes, hospitals, appreciate*) she makes to communicate her insights and understandings. Notice her willingness to explore the spellings of plural endings and possessives.

Let your role be to facilitate students' use of various strategies for spelling unfamiliar words. Record progress by noting increases in written vocabulary (total number of words and number of different words) and in index of control (the percentage of words they can spell conventionally). As you work with young writers, always try to focus on what they can do!

Now consider the writing of six-year-old John who is in an inner-city K–1 classroom. With this new frame, think through the decisions John has made in his writing.

The Sarcise
The Clauns
are
Jagaling
And a Ball
Fell

on the
man that!
tacks the
Ticits And
he could
the PrFesre!
And PrFesre
Fired him! thats a teeralb! thing
the End i Give up i cuit

The list for analysis would look like this:

Conventional Spellings		Constructed Spellings
The, the ~~HH~~	are	Sarcise (*circus*)
And //	a /	Clauns (*clowns*)
Ball	Fell	Jagaling (*juggling*)
on	man	tacks (*takes*)
that	he	Ticits (*tickets*)
Fired	him	could (*called*)
thats	thing	Prfesre (*professor*)
End	i /	teeralb (*terrible*)
Give	up	cuit (*quit*)

A. 37 = # of total words

B. 27 = # of different words

C. 18 = # of different words spelled conventionally

D. 9 = # of different words with constructed spellings

18 divided by 27 = .6666 × 100% = 66.6%

Index of Control = 67%

In this piece it is clear that John sees himself as a writer, as one who uses spelling to communicate his ideas and intentions. It isn't obvious on first glance, however, that John is controlling the spellings of two-thirds of the words he has chosen to use in his writing. He has utilized his knowledge of letter-sound relationships (phonics) to construct or invent spellings for those powerful words he knows belong in his writing. It is important to notice that those words John constructs spellings for are words that might never appear in a spelling program designed for first grade. Words such as *juggling, tickets, professor, terrible,* and *quit* are important to the telling of John's story. These words give the piece a richness and texture that would be absent if John were limited to those words he would have studied in a typical spelling program for first grade. John is encouraged to write what he knows and to use in his writing the same rich language he freely uses in his speech. This attitude frees him to explore and take risks as he gains more and more control over the conventions of written language.

Consider seven-year-old Courtney's writing in the sample below. As a second grader, she has slightly more control over the conventional spellings. Her piece is focused and personal.

I have one sad thing to
say. My grandpa died befor
I was boen so I did't
get to see him I can't stop
thiking about it I ownly
see picshrs of him in
Black and Whight. I would
like to see a picshr of him
in color.

Conventional Spellings		Constructed Spellings
I ⧚	have	befor (*before*)
one	sad	boen (*born*)
thing	to //	did't (*didn't*)
say	My	thiking (*thinking*)
grandpa	died	ownly (*only*)
was	so	picshrs (*pictures*)
get	see //	Whight (*white*)
him //	can't	picshr (*picture*)
stop	about	
it	of /	
in /	Black	
and	would	
like	a	
color		

A. 48 = # of total words

B. 35 = # of different words

C. 27 = # of different words spelled conventionally

D.   8 = # of different words with constructed spellings

27 divided by 35 = .771 × 100% = 77.1%

Index of Control = 77%

Courtney constructs spellings for fewer than one-fourth of the words she chooses to use. Once again, note that the constructed spellings in this piece are for words that are necessary to communicate the very personal message the writer would have imparted through her speech. Courtney, like

Angie and John, has something powerful to say. Notice how her knowledge of letter-sound relationships is evident in her constructions for *pictures*. She uses a known word, *own*, in her construction of "ownly" and visual memory in constructions for *before* ("befor") and *thinking* ("thiking"). Clearly, Courtney is aware of conventional spelling and is working toward greater control. Even so, keep in mind that writers continue to use various strategies for spelling throughout their writing lives.

The last sample in this section was written by seven-year-old Tyler, who is a third-year student in a K–1–2 continuous progress classroom.

The Big haws
Thar was a Big haws and a rath man and the rath man was a
Gete man and he wod mor mane. But the man dod not no the
haws was a magac haws. But own bay the haws sab
to the man you wal see in yowr brens three sparas
tha wal taL you wat wal hpan to you of you bot
shar but the man sab to the haws i wal not
shar my mane but the haws wab not asr sow
the man wab not shar has mane sow the man
Remanb Grete and the Three Sparas cam. The frt spaerat was
the sperat fo lif. Wan he woc up he was scarb
The sperat sab i an the sperat av lif The man stal was scard
The sperat tald the man to cam bawn and the man bab The
sqerat tald the man to fiLo ham and He bab the
sqerat wat to has tim wan the man was
a LataL boy he was rat A math pag. The man
sab thas me yes sab the sperat you ar staeg in be cas
you wr not bueg you math wan you wr spost to
sow you Ar staing in and boweg it Naw we mas Go
Naw and tha Laft wan he woc up thar was No oaE
tar and he wat dac to slep but tan the nas
sperat cam and the man woc up agan the sperat
sab i am the sperat fo sanes folo me the man the sab i
bot wat to The sperat fo sanes dasaperb and the sperat fo bor aperd.
But than the man woc up than the man shard His mane. the End.

58   Spelling in Use

The Big haws   TYLER   ①
Thar Was a Big haws and a nath man and The rath man Was a

·Gofarman and he Wод mд' mane, But the man dd not po The,

haws. Was a magjac haws. But own bay the haws sab

To the man you Wд see In yowr brons Three sparas

Tha Wal tal you Wat Wal hpan To you of you bot

'Shar but The man Sab To the haws i Wal not

Shar my mane but The haWs Wab not asr SoW

the man Wab not Shar has Mane SoW. The man

---

②   TYLER
Remanб Grete and The·Three Sparas cam. The frt spaehat Was

The Sparat fo lif. Wan he Wоc up he WaS Scarb

The Sperat Sab i an The sperat Ov lif The man Stal Was Scand

The Sperat tal The man to cam Lawn and the man bab The

Sqerat Tald The man to filo ham and He bab The

Sqerat Wat to has tim Wan The man Was

a Latal boy he Was rat A math pag. The man

Sab Thas me yes Sab The Sperat you ar stoeg in be cas

TYLER

you wr not bueg yor Math Wan you wr sqost to

sow you Ar staing in and boweg it! Naw we mas Go

Naw and Tha lafit Wan he woc up Thar Was No OaE

Tar and he Wat dac To sleq but tan The nas

sperat cam and the man Woc up agan the sqorat

Sab I am The sperat fo Sanes tolo me the man the Sab I

bot Wat to The sperat fo sapas desoparb and the sperat fo bor aperd

out Than the man Wad up tihan, the man shard His maner the End

(For easier reference, we have listed Tyler's constructed spellings in alphabetical order and have given the number of repetitions in parentheses for his most-repeated words.)

Conventional Spellings

The, the ### ### ### ### ### ### ### (35)

Big /

was ### /// (8)

a ### (5)

and ### ### (10)

man ### ### ### // (17)

he, He ### / (6)

But, but ### (5)

Constructed Spellings

agan (*again*)

an (*am*)

aperd (*appeared*)

ar (*are*) /

asr (*answer*)

av (*of*)

bab (*did*) /

bawn (*down*)

bay (*day*)

Conventional Spellings	Constructed Spellings
not ////	be cas (*because*)
to ⊬ /// (8)	bor (*door*)
you ⊬ // (7)	bot (*don't*) /
see	boweg (*doing*)
in //	brens (*dreams*)
three, Three /	bueg (*doing*)
i ///	cam (*calm*)
my	cam (*came*) /
up ///	dac (*back*)
boy	dasaperb (*disappeared*)
math /	dod (*did*)
me /	fiLo (*follow*)
yes	fo (*of*) ///
it	folo (*follow*)
we	frt (*first*)
Go	Gete (*greedy*)
am	Grete (*greedy*)
His	ham (*him*)
End	has (*his*) /
	haws (*house*) ⊬ / (6)
	hpan (*happen*)
	Laft (*left*)
	LataL (*little*)
	lif (*life*) /
	magac (*magic*)
	mane (*money*) ///
	mas (*must*)
	mor (*more*)

Constructed Spellings

nas (*next*)

naw (*now*) |

no (*know*)

no oaE (*no one*)

of (*if*)

own (*one*)

pag (*page*)

rat (*writing*)

rath (*rich*) |

Remanb (*remained*)

sab (*said*) |||| | (6)

sanes (*science*) |

scarb, scard (*scared*) |

shar (*share*) ||

shard (*shared*)

slep (*sleep*)

sow (*so*) ||

spaerat (*spirit*)

sparas, Sparas (*spirits*) |

sperat, sqerat (*spirit*) |||| |||| |

spost (*supposed*)

staeng (*staying*)

staing (*staying*)

stal (*still*)

taL (*tell*)

tald (*told*) |

tan (*then*)

tar (*there*)

Constructed Spellings

tha (*they*) |

than (*then*) |

thar (*there*) |

thas (*that's*)

the (*then*)

tim (*time*)

wab (*would*) |

wal (*will*) |||

wan (*when*) |||

wat (*want*)

wat (*went*) |

wat (*what*)

woc (*woke*) |||

wod (*wanted*)

wr (*were*) |

yor (*your*)

yowr (*your*)

A. 286 = # of total words

B. 109 = # of different words

C.   27 = # of different words spelled conventionally

D.   82 = # of different words with constructed spellings

27 divided by 109 = .2477 $\times$ 100% = 24.77%

Index of Control = 25%

The one significant difference with this piece is the dramatic
increase in volume. Clearly, Tyler has more to say. Angie was
reporting information she had gained about the nursing pro-
fession. John told of his observations at the circus. Courtney
used writing to express her sadness and longing to meet her
grandfather. Tyler draws upon his imagination, his experience
with story, and his language to create his own tale. Although
he has the lowest index of control, he has the greatest written
verbal fluency—that is, he uses the widest range of words and
does not limit himself to words whose spellings he can control. Tyler's writing reveals that he uses *b* for *d* and reverses *p*,
which might be mistaken for *q*. It is important to look for
these patterns which may be mistaken as error. Tyler's constructions indicate a heavy reliance on letter-sound knowledge and a "spelling-as-it-sounds" strategy. It is this freedom
to construct that enables Tyler to weave his story into a completed fabric. The story reveals knowledge of familiar plots
and character development. The opportunity to work through
this process can only enhance Tyler's overall development as
a writer.

Decide

As teachers research what writers are doing, they use the information they are gathering to make curricular decisions about

what will help writers most at any given time (see vignettes at the end of this chapter for examples of teaching decisions based on observations of writers). These decisions are not based solely on what children are doing. Teachers make decisions about how to help young writers with spelling and all the issues in their writing based on a vision of these children as future writers. These teachers understand how writers deal with spelling (which is often very different from the way schools and programs have dealt with spelling), and they work to keep their curriculum and instruction in line with this understanding. This understanding motivates wise teachers to focus on developing strategic spellers.

To help your understanding of what having a vision for children as writers is all about, consider this story from Katie's life as a writer. Just a few years ago, someone explained to Katie a sensible way to remember whether a word ended in *-ible* or *-able*. When she heard it, Katie thought to herself, "Good. I'll never forget this and I'll never miss these endings again." Today, however, Katie can't tell you the "rule" for remembering this difference. She's forgotten it because she just didn't use it enough. What she hasn't forgotten, though, is that she has a problem with *-ible* and *-able* and, the truth is, this is the more important knowledge for her to have *as a writer*. She knows she needs to check the spellings on words with these endings if she uses them in a high-risk situation.

When we have a vision for children as writers, it must be big enough to consider what kinds of writers they will be, rather than simply what content they need to know. Like all of us, children will forget much of what they don't often use in day to day thinking. What kinds of writers will they be when they've forgotten? Now, let's consider how *writers* deal with spelling.

How Writers Deal with Spelling

- Writers know when they need a strategy other than memory to help them spell a word, and they know which strategies are most useful to help them in these cases. In this way, writers control the conventions of spelling rather than being controlled by those conventions.

- Writers have a sense of their audience and of how high the stakes are (with that audience) for spelling conventionally in their writing. The degree to which writers take measures to check their spelling is related to the stakes involved with various audiences.

- Writers use any words they want to make the clearest expressions in their writing. Writers do not avoid words because they cannot spell them conventionally on their own.

- Writers are also readers who have committed the spellings of many thousands of words to memory and now "own" these conventional spellings as they write (Smith 1988).

- When the audience stakes are high, writers rarely rely solely on their own checking of spelling. They use technology, such as spell-checks, and human resources, such as proofreaders, to help them check for spelling problems.

- Writers do not know how to spell every word they need in their writing.

Teach

Finally, wise teachers help children with their spelling in use. These teachers share strategies with children, point out how one word is spelled differently from a similar word, and *embed talk about spellings* as words are used throughout the day in *meaningful contexts.*

- Mary Ann, a second-grade teacher, reminds her students of that tricky *r* in *"February"* every day for a month (February, of course!) as she opens class with the calendar.

- Bill, a fifth-grade teacher, shares his own spelling strategies (such as *i* before *e*) by demonstrating his thinking when he writes on the board in front of his students.

- Carolyn writes each one of her second-grade students a personal note during the week about how she sees them learning. The notes are precious to the students, as they represent individual attention from the teacher. Embedded in each note are the conventional spellings of a number of words that the students often use when they write back to their teacher.

This sort of spelling instruction isn't usually planned for—it's *anticipated.* Teachers expect "teachable moments" about spelling to arise during the day and they take advantage of them in both individual and whole-class settings.

The content of this "embedded teaching" comes primarily from what teachers know of spelling *as writers themselves* and is therefore focused on the strategies and information about spelling that writers really use as they write. This focus on functional uses keeps spelling in its proper place as a part of writing and allows even the youngest writers to spend their time playing with ideas, not with words. (See Chapter 4 for more examples and vignettes of teaching.)

Teachers who are leading the embedded instruction in spelling for their youngest writers keep reminding their students of the following set of strategies for generating spelling:

- *First, think about how a word looks.* We spell from visual memory more than any other information system. Just as we remember the names of many thousands of objects, people, and places, we remember that *h-o-r-s-e* is *horse* because it looks like that to us and we recognize it immediately, not because we sound it out or decode it.

Help children to draw on this visual memory of words as much as possible. (Smith 1988).

- *Think about whether the word is a long word or a short word.* Often, children don't think about the proportional relationship of letters to word length. You don't want to spell *Tyrannosaurus rex* with only two letters or *leg* with seven!

- *Is the word like any other words you know?* If so, make connections in the spellings. Watch for these connections when looking at pieces of writing because they are often the child's theory base for many constructed spellings.

- *Is the word written nearby?* We don't want to see children struggle to write *Saturday* when there's a calendar hanging just above them! Teachers do have to keep an eye on how environmental print is being used, though. If children are overrelying on it—not wanting to write any words unless they can find the correct spelling for them somewhere—they will not be growing in their ability to generate the spellings they need.

- *Think about what sounds you hear in the word.* Emphasize this point last. It has often been said that the worst spellers are the "wuns ho spel fonetikaly." We need to teach children to "sound out" words, stretching them like rubber bands and listening to the different sound parts. We must also remember, however, that this is often the least efficient way to generate a conventional spelling.

The success of these or any spelling strategies lies in children using them wisely, drawing on the first one most and the others only when extra help is needed. Through observation, questioning, and analysis of writing samples, teachers can get a sense of how children are using various strategies to spell as they write.

Vignettes: Kelvin, Paola, and Christina

Kelvin

Kelvin's kindergarten teacher usually had good success with figuring out the sensible ways her beginning writers were spelling, but Kelvin was an anomaly for her. There seemed to be little or no visual or phonetic correspondence between the words Kelvin would write and the words he would read as his writing. Kelvin's illustrations were quite detailed and often in-cluded conventional environmental print, showing that Kelvin used his visual memory extensively in his artwork, unlike his words. Kelvin was also making very good progress in reading, again relying on both visual memory and letter-sound corre-spondences to help him figure out text. When the teacher

Kelvin's story about his trip to the Gap.

asked Kelvin how he thought of how to write the words, Kelvin repeatedly said, "I just think of them." Kelvin read the piece pictured on page 67 to his teacher as, "My mom took me to Gap and bought me a new green shirt."

Kelvin's teacher decided to observe him as he wrote one morning to see if there were any clues to this anomaly in his actions as a writer. As she watched, she noticed that Kelvin first drew his picture, paying close attention to many small details in backgrounds and figures. When the picture was finished, Kelvin began to write. His teacher noticed him looking around the room after placing each letter in the text. She began to follow the line of his vision and noticed that Kelvin looked at the sign that said *library* and then wrote an *l*. Next, he looked at the word *April* on a calendar and wrote the letter *a*. This pattern

Kelvin's story about his trip to the beach.

continued as the teacher watched Kelvin find words in the room, take a letter (usually the beginning one) from each one and add it to his paper!

Wisely, Kelvin's teacher taught *into* his process, confirming that it was helpful to use environmental print but showing him a better way to do this. She also showed him the other strategies, especially emphasizing thinking about how a word looks because she knew Kelvin had very strong visual memory (she'd seen this in his illustrations). Literally overnight, Kelvin, his teacher, and his classmates could start to read his writing because he had learned to draw on new strategies as a writer.

Kelvin wrote the piece pictured on page 68, "Me my mom and my dad and brother went to the beach," just three days after this powerful conference with his teacher. Notice the typical pattern of strong approximations of spelling early in the piece and then a falling away from this strength toward the end, as Kelvin gets tired. The new work of deeply theoretical generated spelling is hard and tiring, and we often see this falling away near the end of young writers' early pieces.

Paola

Rising to the expectations of her kindergarten teacher, Paola saw herself as a writer and went happily to the writing workshop each day. She wrote about things that were happening in her life and, though shy, she would share her writing with the children sitting close to her. In the piece on page 70, she writes about her family at Christmas, reading it as, "We got a lot of presents for Christmas for fun." At this point in the year, Paola was writing letters that she knew, but not yet making many letter-sound connections.

In early spring, Paola's teacher decided to help her young writers by having each of them make dictionary boxes of their favorite words to use in their writing. Soon after, Paola's writing took a major turn. She was still writing about the same topics in her life, but she had lost faith in her ability to

Paola's story about Christmas with her family.

write the words she needed, and she began to rely exclusively on her box of words, losing all meaningful (syntax, semantics, pragmatics) word-to-message relationships. In the
next piece pictured, notice that if you simply looked at the
number of conventionally spelled words, fourteen out of fif-
teen are correctly spelled. Of course, together they don't
mean anything! Paola read the piece on page 71 to her
teacher as, "My sister and I went to the park to play."

Paola's teacher realized that the box of correct spellings
had heightened Paola's awareness of convention to a point
where she had lost faith in her own abilities as a writer. The
teacher began to notice that other children, though they did
not go to the extremes that Paola did, were mostly writing
about whatever topics could be handled with the words in
their boxes. After an honest conversation with her students
about how she felt the word boxes were hurting them more

CAt . ZOO   frog fox

PenciL LiOn

rAInbow nose nAbbit

hnistmAs Spning

dog down red hoc

A piece written while Paola was relying on her dictionary box.

than helping them as writers, Paola's teacher ceremoniously allowed the children who wanted to get rid of the boxes to do so and go back to making sense of spelling without them. After an individual conference with her teacher, Paola dramatically returned to the sensible strategies she had used before the word box. Notice that in her next piece, written just a week later than the "Cat, zoo . . ." piece, Paola has used several spelling strategies as she writes, "When I went outside I saw flowers." With experience, Paola has grown so much as a reader and writer since Christmas!

Paola describing flowers she'd seen.

Christina

Though the writing of Christina, a first grader, showed an obvious attention to how words sound, her teacher was concerned that this young writer might be relying too heavily on this one spelling strategy because she was not seeing the growth toward conventional spelling that she expected in a writer as fluent as Christina. By observing Christina writing the following piece, her teacher noticed that Christina wrote very quickly and that her mouth moved constantly, shaping the sounds as she went. It was apparent that Christina's pencil could not keep up with her "sounding out," because many words had significantly fewer letters than convention would dictate. Christina was relying exclusively on one strategy as she wrote—"sounding out." Christina read the first of her pictured pieces as, "When it's the last day of school I'm going to Florida. I get to see my family. It's going to take a long time." We suspect, however, that when she first generated the text, the last words were *two days* rather than *a long time*. She remembered what they meant—two days is a long time—but found reading them as she'd written them to be difficult.

Christina's story about a summer trip to Florida.

Christina's teacher sat beside her, confirmed her thinking about the sounds of words as a good strategy, patiently again showed Christina how to use the other spelling strategies (visual cues, word length, etc.), and suggested she make spaces between her words when she wrote. Her next pictured piece shows dramatic growth as Christina goes to her writing with a more sophisticated repertoire of strategies at her disposal. You will notice again the falling away from strong approximation (as in the writings of Paola and Kelvin) as Christina gets

Christina's story about an upcoming trip to the zoo.

tired near the end. Christina read this piece as, "I am going to the zoo with my class. And I am going to see the animals. I am going to eat my lunch. My mom is going with me. Then I'm going home. I'll fall asleep. Then I'll wake up again."

CHAPTER 4

Structures and Routines: Classroom Possibilities

One of the primary concerns shared by many teachers in transition from a spelling textbook to a study of spelling in use is the use of time. The structures and routines of the textbook are so clear-cut, decisions are made, and options are delineated. Moving to a more balanced literacy program, where writing is the focus and spelling is studied in use, can be intimidating to some teachers. As you are developing the professional knowledge base necessary for teaching into what the children are trying to do in their writing and language use, you may find it helpful to see what others have done in their own transition.

Many teachers are familiar with the typical class period for the textbook approach to spelling. In this piece we will suggest a set of predictable structures that you may find useful as you move away from the textbook and begin to deal with spelling in use. We recommend that children be given at least one hour a day to work as writers. In this hour, a number of predictable things might happen, but the mainstays of the writing workshop are *whole-group meetings, writing,* and *whole-* or *small-group share sessions.*

Whole-Group Meeting (5 to 10 minutes)

The teacher directs a mini-lesson, students are gathered and listening, teacher is *teaching*. Mini-lessons focus on many different aspects of writing, of which spelling may be a small but significant part. Possibilities include the following scenarios:

- The teacher writes in front of the students and thinks aloud as she generates spellings, giving access to her thinking about spelling.

- The teacher leads an inquiry into spelling patterns and/or anomalies such as *ed* endings, doubling final consonants, vowel pairs, and homophones. Over several days (typically), students look for these patterns as they write and read and experience the print in their environment. The patterns are collected and categorized, and students generate theories about the spelling patterns.

- The teacher shows students how to use a spelling strategy such as "have a go," where a writer tries spelling a difficult word two or three different ways and selects the one that looks most right. Other strategies are described throughout this book.

Writing (30 to 40 minutes)

Children are writing (reading and talking as needed to support their writing) while the teacher confers with individuals and small groups, teaching them the strategies and skills they need for the work at hand. Possibilities include the following scenarios:

- Children are writing in many different genres, such as poetry, fantasy, memoir, and informational writing. They are also writing in personal journals, notebooks, and learning logs. The teacher emphasizes different stakes for conventional spellings based on audience and stages of drafts, yet encourages writers to be attentive to their growing understanding of the conventions of writing.

- The teacher confers individually and with small groups of children about their writing. She uses these conferences to teach directly into the children's writing. This teaching may include spelling strategies or patterns that a child needs while in the process of writing.

Whole-Group or Small-Group Share Session (5 to 10 minutes)

Selected students are teaching from their strategies. The selected students teach, the teacher listens, other children listen and question.

Possibilities include the following scenarios:

- The teacher encourages children to make note of spellings that interest them when they read, write, and explore the print in their environments. When the class comes together for a share session, children may offer the spelling anomalies they found for others to consider. This helps children realize the fact that our language is meaning based and alphabetic, but not necessarily phonetic (Smith 1985; Goodman 1993; Mills, O'Keefe, and Stephens 1992).

- As the teacher confers with the students, she looks for individuals who can share their strategies with the class later.

Mini-lessons

Most of the direct instruction in spelling occurs in the mini-lessons. These may be for the whole group when the teacher decides that a strategy is one that will be of benefit to the entire writing community. More often, however, mini-lessons will be directed to small groups and individuals as the teacher confers with children about their writing. In most cases the mini-lessons focus on strategies such as those identified by Sandra Wilde and Christine Bouffler, and described in Chapter 1. A mini-lesson might address such specific skills as when and how to use contractions, how to make plurals, how and when to add *ed*, strategies for remembering how to spell words such as *separate*, and *dessert*, and other words which children repeatedly tend to find difficult. For accountability purposes teachers make a note of all the lessons they teach, whether they be with groups or individuals. Mini-lessons can focus on *strategies, spelling patterns* and *rules*, and even *gimmicks* that help writers generate spellings. Some examples of each type of mini-lessons follow; also see *You Kan Red This* (Wilde 1992) for other useful strategies, patterns, and rules.

Strategy.   Beverly, a fifth-grade teacher, speaks to a small group of her students. "I've noticed," she says, "that when you guys are writing your drafts, you spend a lot of time looking up words you don't know how to spell. Let me make a suggestion. When I'm writing and I'm unsure of a spelling, I often write it on a Post-it™ note two or three different ways and go with the one that looks most right to me. This saves me time while I'm drafting, and I always know I can go back again later if I'm still unsure. So, will you guys try this out for a few days and let me know how it's working for you? If you like it, we can share it with the rest of the class—maybe on Friday."

Other examples:

- If you are having trouble with a spelling, try to remember what the word looks like.

- Before you finish a writing project, have someone else help you check your spellings.

Patterns and Rules.   Kevin, a second-grade teacher, gathers his whole class around him. "I need to show all of you how to do something in your spelling. Many of you use words that end in *ing* like *having* and *taking* and *giving*." Kevin writes these words on the board. He asks his students, "What were these words before we added the *ing* to them?" Quickly, several students answer with the correct root words. "Did you notice," Kevin asks, "that the final *e* is dropped off each one before we add the *ing*?" This is something you can usually count on in your writing—that you need to drop the final *e* on a word when you add *ing*. Will you help each other to remember that as you're writing? I'll leave these examples posted on our chart for a while just to help you."

Other examples:

- plural endings

- adding prefixes and suffixes

- possessive forms

- contractions

Gimmick.   Mary Ann, a third-grade teacher, is discussing a draft of a letter that three of her students have written to the principal. She notices the word *separate* spelled as "seperate" in their draft. She exclaims, "Oh, *separate*! I used to misspell this word all the time until someone told me to remember that there was 'a rat' in the middle of that word, and I've never forgotten that it's *arate* instead of *erate*." Maybe that will help you. Will one of you tell the class about this quickly when we meet for our share session later?"

Other examples:

- A double helping of dessert gives you two *s*'s in this word.

- The princi*pal* is your pal.

From Spelling Instruction to Spelling Inquiry

In a more traditional approach to spelling instruction, the structures and routines are dictated by an arbitrary scope and sequence determined by distant and unseen "experts." Curricular and instructional decisions are never left to the teacher, the one person who has the most intimate knowledge of the readers and writers in the classroom. When spelling instruction is a matter of moving the children through the spelling book, teachers do not have to make any decisions about what to teach and when to teach it. However, when writing is the focus and spelling instruction is an embedded part of that focus, teachers must rely on their own knowledge of spelling in use. That knowledge comes from their own experiences as writers and kidwatchers, as well as from professional resources, and it is refined through reflective practice.

Other than direct teaching, a balanced literacy program requires a supportive classroom environment. Such an environment would be rich with print. This could include menus, schedules, color words, numbers, directions, mailboxes, the alphabet, a calendar, instructions, a class list, sign-up sheets, books (organized by author, genre, title, topic), maps, address book, a return address for the classroom, and any other print that would support the work of young readers and writers. In addition to environmental print, writers will need resources such as dictionaries, spell-checks, and computers to support their spelling growth. Naturally, decisions about what to include in the environment would be made on the basis of the age and development of the children. Learning to use the sources in the room is a valuable strategy to any young writer.

Many teachers who work with spelling in use daily in their writing workshops also make time during the week to lead a spelling inquiry in their classrooms. This time is in addition to, not in place of, the predictable writing workshop. These teachers want to encourage their young writers to be curious about words and to have a respect for the language they will use to fill their lives with powerful writing. Three of these spelling inquiry structures are described below. What is important about each of these structures in classrooms is that the focus remains on the children as writers. The spelling curriculum that is "covered" in these structures is generated from the work children do and the questions they have as writers and readers.

Spelling Inquiry #1: A Third-Grade Classroom

A block of time on Thursday mornings in a third-grade classroom in New York City is reserved for spelling study. This focus time on spelling is a predictable structure in this classroom, and the students prepare for it all week long. Their preparation, however, is not in the form of spelling exercises or drills on lists of words. These third graders prepare by living their lives as writers with a curiosity about and a respect for words. When the focus time on spelling begins, the writers gather, with their notebooks or small scraps of paper in hand.

During the week the teacher asks his students to live with two questions in their writing lives in preparation for spelling study time. One question is, "What words have you written this week that were hard for you or made you wonder about their spellings?" The other question is, "What words have you read this week whose spellings made you curious?" The students are to collect such words during the week (no set number of them) and bring them to the Thursday morning spelling study time.

Using the words his students bring in, the teacher leads the group into inquiry about spelling patterns, meaning-based relationships in spelling, and spelling anomalies. Because he has created this open-ended structure for the study of spelling in his classroom, the teacher must be ready to "teach into" what his young writers bring. He brings a great deal of knowledge about spelling to his student in these sessions. For example, when one student is curious about *ph* spelling the *f* sound in many words, the teacher explains that *phon* means *sound* and that's why many words use that letter combination—because of what they mean, not how they sound. The students think of all the words they can that have the *ph* combination as they use the teacher's information to test out this meaning relationship. They find exceptions, of course, but they are used to exceptions in this kind of inquiry. In addition to explaining to the students many things about spelling as they bring words to study, the teacher also frequently explains his own thought process to them when faced with a spelling anomaly.

Over the course of the year, the teacher and his students often get "on about" something in their spelling inquiry and stay with it over time—as they did with the pattern *ough*. For several days, the students collected words with this pattern and charted them by sound as they worked to develop a theory about this unusual pattern. The teacher also makes books about spelling available to his students (including teacher's resource books, such as Sandra Wilde's *You Kan Red This*), and the students often look to these resources when they are interested in particular patterns or meaning relationships.

What Is Significant About This Structure?

- There is no set curriculum for which words to focus on or what to study about spelling.

- Children learn a great deal of content knowledge about spelling, but this content (curriculum) is clearly generated by the work students do as writers.

- The emphasis in this spelling program is on children's habits of mind—being curious about words. The emphasis is not on specific pieces of information about spelling or specific words.

- The spelling study time is predictable so that students can expect it and live toward it in their thinking. The students have a great deal of responsibility in making this inquiry relevant and interesting.

- The inquiry approach to spelling helps the student understand the complexity of spelling. Students may be more willing to take risks because the emphasis is not on holding correct spellings for mastery tests.

- The theory building and searching out of patterns in the inquiry approach helps children to be more aware of patterns and apply this to their spelling in use.

Outline of This Predictable Structure

- There is predictable weekly time for spelling inquiry in the classroom. This block of time would usually be about thirty minutes in length and should be in addition to the writing workshop time, not in place of it. When the class is really excited about something in spelling inquiry, there may be short follow-up gatherings during the week as students find new examples of patterns or have new insights.

- During the week, teachers ask students to make a note of words whose spellings are difficult or interesting to them. Students find these words as they engage in their own writing and reading. Teachers may want to require that these noted words be turned in each week, but this is not necessary. The teacher can certainly ask about noted words from time to time in conferences with individual students and might even ask upper-grade students to report on their own individual spelling inquiries.

- We recommend that teachers *not* set a certain quantity of words for students to find for inquiry each week. If the focus is on genuine inquiry, the words will present themselves—sometimes several in a week for a student, sometimes none at all.

- When the whole class comes together to study spelling, the teacher may need a structure for determining who contributes the words for study, although this is not necessary. If a structure is needed, the teacher might divide the class into groups who meet briefly to discuss the words they have collected; the teacher then may ask one of these groups to bring the words or word patterns for that week's study.

- We recommend that there be no spelling tests of any kind in this structure. Since the point of this approach to the study of spelling is to teach children to be curious about words as they grow in their knowledge of words, there is no need for them to demonstrate mastery of specific words on tests.

Spelling Inquiry #2: A Kindergarten Classroom

During the class meeting on Monday morning in a kindergarten classroom, the teacher carefully uncovers a picture that has been taped to or drawn on the top of a large piece of chart paper. This morning, the picture is of an elephant. The teacher pronounces the word "*elephant.*" The children look at it carefully and immediately begin to think about it. These young writers know that sometime during the day they will come to this chart either alone or with a friend and generate a spelling for this word, *elephant.*

Throughout the day the chart fills with various attempts at this spelling, each one signed by the writer who "had a go." The first writers to try a spelling take the biggest risk, as they create a forum for discussion for those who follow. The teacher loves to listen in on the talk during the day that surrounds the attempts to spell the word. By listening in, she is able to learn a great deal about what strategies her students are using to generate spellings, and she notes the insight she gains as a reminder for future mini-lessons or individual conferences.

Near the end of the day, the class comes together again around the chart with the elephant at the top, but this time the children gather as researchers, as their teacher has taught them to be. She has them look for patterns in the various attempts, such as every try having an *l* and an *f* somewhere in the word. They discuss the patterns they see, and some children talk through how they generated their spellings. The teacher listens carefully and teaches into any strategies that should be confirmed, even though sometimes the smart strategies do not render the conventional spelling.

Such was the case with this word, *elephant,* as children described hearing an *f* and so they wrote *f* in the word. The teacher confirms that matching the sounds you hear to the letters you know is a smart thing to do, especially for very young writers. One child put two *l*'s in his attempt because, he said, "I was thinking that a lot of words have two *l*'s together in the middle and it looked like this one should have two." Again, the teacher confirms that thinking about how parts of this word might be like parts of other words you've seen is a smart strategy. "But," she says with a smile on her face, "*elephant* is a tricky one," and she goes on to show the children the conventional spelling and talk to them about the various parts of the words, teaching content about letter patterns as she does. Because of all the early confirmations and the general tone of the inquiry that the teacher creates, the children do not seem at all defeated when their teacher shows them the conventional spelling. Instead, they seem very curious and think of themselves as quite smart for getting as close as they did. They often have a good laugh about the words that trick them with silent letters or unexpected patterns.

What's Significant About This Structure?

- This structure was chosen for this kindergarten classroom for several reasons, but one of them is the most critical in the teacher's mind. This structure creates a *climate of trying* in the classroom. These children know what to do when they come to a word that's hard for them because they do it routinely as a class structure. They also know that even nonconventional spellings can be very smart choices when they are theory based (an expression the teacher uses with her students). So the words and the patterns they present are less important to the teacher than the fact that her students learn to try and feel comfortable with attempting to spell words that are new or difficult for them. The focus is on the children as writers.

- The teacher must be a careful listener throughout the day and during the children's gathering as researchers around the chart. She is listening for the smart ways her students are thinking so she can confirm these, and she's also listening for what it seems they don't yet know so she can teach them. We call this "teaching into" a generated curriculum.

- The teacher encourages her students to attempt the spelling with a friend because she trusts that the talk that is generated in their interactions will be very instructional. She wants students to learn from each other so she makes it a part of the structure.

- The teacher wants her young writers to understand what it means to approximate spelling and why they need to be willing to use approximation as writers. This structure helps her children to understand approximation, as it draws their attention to the intelligence shown in their attempts but still acknowledges the fact that they are approximating (by showing them the conventional spelling). The teacher uses the word *convention* routinely with her kindergarten students because she wants them to understand what it means and how they will grow toward it in her classroom. This wise teacher doesn't hide her instructional theory base from her students, but shares it with them.

Outline of This Predictable Structure

- The teacher reveals a pictured word somewhere in the room and pronounces it.

- There can be many reasons for choosing a pictured word: A student may suggest one, the teacher may see a need to look at a certain pattern in the children's writing, or the curriculum from another part of the day may suggest a word. Remember that the primary goal of the structure is to teach the strategies of approximation for young writers, so the words can come from anywhere.

- Children come up alone or in pairs during the day and approximate a spelling for the word. Their only resource for this approximation is their brains. Some teachers use this structure all in one sitting, passing out note cards to pairs for their written approximations, and then collecting the cards and studying them as a group.

- The teacher first listens as children talk about how they generated their spellings, and she confirms any smart strategies she hears them explaining.

- The teacher reveals the conventional spelling and explains it in terms of letter-sound relationships, letter patterns, meaning base, and similarities to other words.

The teacher encourages the children to ask questions as they examine the conventional spellings.

- Sometimes children will generate the conventional spellings in their attempts. Though this is worth a celebration, the teacher must lead the way in showing that the conventional spelling was not the only smart one generated.

- The teacher should keep records of the words the class has attempted to spell and retrace patterns from time to time in new words to show the children how to transfer their growing knowledge bases to new approximations.

CHAPTER 5

Communicating with Parents

The teaching of spelling in use *looks* very different from what many people are used to seeing in classroom spelling instruction. For many parents, walking down the halls of an elementary school where children's real attempts at writing are celebrated and displayed can be a disconcerting experience at best. "Aren't they teaching them anything?" is the question that comes to mind for many. Because they lack the knowledge base to understand what they are seeing, these parents would likely be much happier if they saw row after row of conventional, neatly copied "stories" on display. For this reason, teachers who choose a spelling in use curricular and instructional approach will have to communicate regularly with parents to help them understand how their children are being helped to become better writers (and spellers!). From the beginning of the teacher/parent relationship, it is important to stress the belief that you are not preparing children to someday be writers, you are allowing them to be writers now. This means that they will write like the children they are, six-year-olds making daily discoveries about a fascinating, complex language that gives them power and voice. In this chapter we provide practical help in communicating with parents about the teaching of spelling in use. The chapter covers four areas—workshops for parents,

conferences with parents, individual letters to parents, and
classroom newsletters. The chapter ends with a summary of
the information we often share with parents in newsletter formats. As you read this chapter we encourage you to think
about ways to extend your classroom and make it an inviting
place for parents to learn alongside their children.

The Parent Workshop

One effective way to communicate with parents is to present a
workshop on spelling. Your workshop can demonstrate to parents how children develop as writers and how spelling knowledge emerges and is constructed through experience and
instruction.

Goals

However you decide to conduct your workshop for parents,
you may find it helpful to consider the following goals in the
planning phase:

- to examine the developmental nature of spelling as part
  of the child's overall literacy development

- to introduce strategies that facilitate development in
  spelling

- to introduce a system of record keeping that documents
  spelling growth and change

- to introduce the concept that instruction in spelling
  does not mean slavishly following a spelling textbook

- to help parents understand that you see children's conventional approximations as opportunities for you to

teach, not reasons to penalize children for what they do not yet understand

Examining the developmental nature of spelling as a part of the child's overall literacy development. You might use samples of children's writing such as those presented in Chapter 1 to demonstrate how the instructional practice in the classroom influences writing. You might also show how a focus on spelling in use can lead to more fluent writing. These samples, or ones from your own students, can be used to help parents understand how the skills they value (letter formation, spacing, punctuation, sentence structure) are not ignored when emphasis is given to expressing the writer's knowledge, feelings, and questions.

You could present Cambourne's conditions for learning (as outlined in Chapter 1) and show how the classroom environment you and the children have established maximizes those conditions. Use examples from the daily routine (as presented in Chapter 4) to demonstrate how these conditions are created, and show their connections to the writing samples you share.

Introducing strategies that facilitate spelling development. You could present the spelling strategies by Sandra Wilde described earlier and demonstrate to parents how all writers (even adults) employ various strategies to generate spelling. You might have parents brainstorm all the things they usually do when they are writing and are uncertain about how to spell a particular word. We find that the strategies adults use most often will easily fall within the five strategies Wilde has identified. It is often enlightening for parents to realize that learning one strategy that can be used in many contexts is more efficient than memorizing the single spellings of countless words children may or may not use in their writing. You could do the same with the ten strategies Bouffler outlined (see Chapter 1). This may help parents understand the strategies we are working toward with our students. However, it is important to emphasize that our youngest writers will only approximate the use of these strategies, as they have ownership over far fewer words than a more mature writer.

Introducing a system of record keeping that documents spelling growth and change.   You may find it useful to use the information in Chapter 3 to show how you will make instructional decisions and document growth and development. Samples from a child's writing folder that demonstrate the wise things the child has done, over time, to generate the spellings needed to communicate his or her intentions can help parents see the power of having a repertoire of spelling strategies. Being able to inform parents about a child's developing control over strategies (using the notion of an index of control) can help parents understand that spelling tests are not the only devices to determine whether their children are learning to spell. In fact, parents may come to understand that spelling tests are very poor measures of a child's spelling in use.

Introducing the notion that instruction in spelling does not mean slavishly following a spelling textbook.   You may find it helpful to share your vision for instruction in spelling as a part of the overall writing/literacy curriculum. You could present for parents some examples of the predictable structures and routines that will be present in the classroom you share with their children (as described in Chapter 4). Demonstrate what will occur in a mini-lesson and explain how you decide what to teach and to whom. Review the classroom stories found in Chapter 4, and use examples from your own class to show how you have established expectations for your students. This can help parents to understand that instruction in spelling occurs both directly and indirectly in a holistic writing curriculum. Parents can come to appreciate inquiry, mini-lessons, group share sessions, and various other strategies as valuable instruction.

Helping parents understand that children's approximations are teaching opportunities, not reasons to penalize children for what they do not yet understand.   Most parents have a history of schooling which taught them that all errors in learning were to be penalized with poor grades, rewritten work, or extra "practice." You will have to help parents to see that you use children's approximations ("errors") as curricular information from which you make plans about how to teach a child. The moves children make with language give us windows into what they understand and what they need to know. We need children to show us what they need to know, so we must reduce the stakes for taking risks in their learning.

Parent Workshop Ideas

The following are workshop ideas that we have used with groups of parents to generate conversations about spelling that lead to an understanding of the insights outlined above.

- Find a word in the dictionary that you do not expect most parents to know—a word like *branchiopodan*. Pronounce the word several times and give the definition. Then ask parents to generate a spelling for the word. Compare the different possibilities and have parents talk about how they generated these possibilities. The conversation about this activity should help parents to see that generating spellings for words we don't know causes us to draw on knowledge of letter-sound relationships, knowledge of meaning units, and knowledge of letter patterns—all of which come from what we know about other words. Use this conversation to explain how you work on building up these knowledge bases in your spelling program rather than on focusing on individual words. Emphasize the importance of reading in building up a visual history with words.

- Explain to parents that the average literate adult can generate correct spellings for between forty and fifty thousand words (Smith 1988). Point out that many of these words are ones that have never actually been used in writing by the adult, yet the conventional spellings can be generated. Have parents discuss how this much knowledge about spelling could have happened, and use this conversation to help them understand that adults did not learn these words one at a time. Help them to see that adults have learned to spell from reading and writing (Smith 1988) and that they draw on a vast visual history of having seen words spelled for them as they read. This will help you support the fact that you are teaching children to spell whenever they are engaged in reading and writing.

- Have parents think about their vision for their child as a writer—say, ten years from now. How do they hope their child will be as a writer in the future? Included in this, of course, is how this child will deal with spelling. This conversation should help parents to see that the ultimate goal is that the child be conscientious about taking his or her writing into the world, not holding the correct spelling for every single word the child will ever encounter. Be very clear with parents about your vision for their child as a writer, and show them specifically how you are helping that vision become a reality. Dealing with conventional spelling is part of a much bigger vision, and parents should know this.

- Have parents of upper-grade students think about how their own writing processes change, depending on their intended audience. Have them imagine the different processes involved in writing a letter to a relative, a memo to a boss, and an application for a job. Help them to understand that the writing process—and, in particular how writers deal with something like spelling—is not the same for every audience. Explain to parents that you talk to your students a lot about making the writing process fit the stakes of the audience. For high-stakes audiences, you have students take fewer risks and double-check their conventional spelling and usage with their peers. For low-stakes audiences, they can take more risks and worry far less about "looking dumb" because of their conventional spelling and usage. In your classroom, show parents how you have children engage in a range of writing for different high- and low-stakes audiences.

- To help parents understand the role of reading and visual memory in remembering spellings (Smith 1988), you might draw a picture of a horse on the board and ask parents what this "says." They'll say, "*horse*," of course. Then quickly write the word *horse* and ask them what it says. They'll say, "*horse*," of course! They won't "sound out" to get this word, they won't imagine other similar words, they won't even think about meaningful units of the word—they'll simply know it looks like *horse* in the same way the picture looked like a horse. In many ways, the alphabet allows us to "draw pictures" of words with letters. As readers and writers, remembering what the "letter pictures" of words look like helps us to read and spell them, as Smith so eloquently helps us to understand. This will help parents understand the critical role of extensive reading in learning to spell: children learn to recognize the words they read repeatedly (just as they recognize objects in their environments), and they recreate these recognized words as they write.

Helping Children at Home with Spelling

The following ideas could be shared with parents to encourage them to work at home with their children if they are especially concerned about spelling growth.

- Parents of young children can place plastic magnetic letters on the refrigerator and encourage their children to make words, as well as make words themselves. "I Love You" is an easy message to leave. Kids can use the letters to tell what they would like to have for dinner!

- Encourage parents to have written conversations with their child. After parents see the conditions that help children to learn through demonstration, they should understand the value of the written conversation. You may suggest that parents keep a journal for these conversations so that their child's growth can be traced over time, creating a beautiful family artifact. Be sure that before these written conversations are under way, the parents understand and value their child's constructed spellings.

- Suggest that parents have a regular message board in their homes where all members of the family (even the youngest writers) leave and receive messages. Again, be sure before you suggest this that you have helped parents value learning through demonstration and their child's constructed spellings.

- Encourage parents to give "literary gifts" to their child—books, pens, a variety of paper, stationery, little poems for little pockets, blank books, etc. A great birthday gift for a young writer is a box full of paper, stickers, and things to write with—a writer's box!

- Encourage parents to have their child write for many different purposes and audiences. Children should write notes to remind parents of things they want, thank-you letters to friends and relatives, stories and cards as presents for others, and even letters of complaint to officials when they are upset about things they see as unfair.

- Suggest that parents engage their child in an inquiry about a word pattern that makes them curious. For example, the family might start a chart on the refrigerator of all the words they can think of that have the long *e* sound in them and then study all the different ways this sound can be spelled.

- Encourage parents to demonstrate a curiosity about words as they travel with their child down the interstate, or to the grocery store, the mall, or a restaurant, or just when they read aloud with their child. When parents comment on an interesting word or a spelling anomaly, they not only draw attention to the word or letter pattern but also demonstrate that readers and writers are curious about words.

- Emphasize to parents that reading is the best teacher of writing and spelling (Smith 1988). Parents should be sure that their children have access to many books and should encourage their children to read often.

Conferences with Parents

Another powerful line of communication with parents about your curriculum and instruction is the parent conference. Too often, teachers and parents only schedule conferences together when there is some problem. However, in classrooms where spelling and other content is taught in use in children's writing, conferences are one of the best ways to help parents know how curriculum and instruction are being generated by their child's work and how their child is growing as a writer. The conference allows the teacher to explain in detail both how he or she is working individually with the child and how he or she is teaching the whole class. The conference also lets parents ask questions that will help them understand and feel comfortable with the instruction that may look very different from what they expect to happen in school. Parents should be issued an ongoing, open invitation to confer with the teacher about their child's work.

The following are some suggestions we have found useful in dealing with parents when one of our primary concerns was to help parents understand how we teach spelling and other content in use in children's writing.

- Before the conference begins, review samples of the child's work and have these ready for the parents to see. Using Post-it™ notes or some other flagging system, mark places in the child's work that are significant indicators of growth in writing. For example, you might mark a piece that has several examples of silent letters represented in spellings to show movement toward visual memory and ownership of spellings. Many parents will not know what signs to look for to see growth.

- Show parents any in-process notes you have taken about the child's writing. Explain how you study the child's work and use that information to make curricular decisions. Report on the conferences you have had with the child that were a result of your study of that child's writing. Understanding that you are familiar with each student's work will help parents value your instruction because it is so like what parents do as they help children learn and grow at home.

- Have records of the content you have taught in minilessons to the whole class ready for parents to see. The mini-lesson is most like what parents expect to be happening in the classroom, and it can be a bridge they can meet you on as they come to understand your teaching of spelling in use. Be sure to explain how you decide which mini-lessons to teach to the whole class.

- If you are giving grades for spelling, the parent conference is the place where you should explain to parents exactly how this is done. If you are not giving grades for spelling but are giving grades for writing, explain how spelling figures into that grade. If, as we hope, you do not have to deal with grades at all and you instead describe children's development as writers when you report to parents, explain how you track a child's growth over time. You will want to mention both records of conferences with the child and samples of work with analyses like those mentioned in Chapter 3.

- Open up the conference generally and frequently for parents' questions. You should also ask parents leading questions about their children that communicate your vision for the classroom and that teach parents to think about their child's writing in new ways. For example, after parents have looked through their child's samples, you might ask them which piece of writing they think represents the greatest risk taking by their child. You might ask parents to tell you about their child's interest in writing and words at home. You might simply ask parents what they can tell you about their child as a learner that will help you teach their child better. By getting parents to talk about their child's learning, you help them to see that you care about that child as an individual. This is a powerful thing for parents to understand.

- Be sure to end the conference by telling parents where you next plan to focus your attention, with regard to their child's development as a writer. Show them how you made this focused decision and how it came from a combination of a vision you have for their child as a writer and an understanding of where that child is at this time in his or her growth.

- The bottom line when conferring with parents is to communicate that you are doing your best to teach their child, not just as one of a group of thirty children, but as a writer in his or her own right. Help parents to see that it is difficult, complicated work, but that you are willing to do it.

Letters to Parents

As suggested above, we recommend that teachers find many forums for communicating with parents, such as workshops, newsletters, and conferences about a child's work. We make one further recommendation—that letters to parents *be individualized for each child* in the classroom. General information about curriculum and instruction can be shared in a standard newsletter format, but the more specific report of a child's growth toward spelling in use should be done on a child-by-child basis. Growth in a child's writing over time is not a unique phenomenon, but it is an individual one; at any given moment in the classroom, each child will be experiencing that individual growth as a writer. If we choose to refocus our writing curriculum so that we deal with spelling in use, we must find a way to let parents know how each child is using spelling in his or her writing and how this is a part of the child's overall growth as a writer. As parents and teachers, we are convinced that there is no more powerful communication between home and school than a personalized note about one child's development.

In the busyness of our teaching lives, however, we must remember to keep our teaching manageable, and so we offer some suggestions to help with the management of individualized parent letters. Following these suggestions are a few sample letters to parents that might accompany children's writing samples.

- Keep the letters short and to the point. The fact that the letter to parents is about only their child is what will make it powerful, not its length.

- Inform parents in a newsletter or a school meeting that they can expect these letters about their child's growth. This will keep parents from seeing the letters as an indication that something is wrong (the old reason that individual letters were sent home).

- Pace yourself. Plan to write only four or five letters to parents a week. Again, the individualized letter is powerful because it's individualized, and the quality of that negates the need for quantity. You might set a goal of, say, five individualized letters to each child's parents during the school year.

- If at all possible, use a word processor to write individualized letters. You can save them, spell-check them, and, in general, write the letters much more quickly on a word processor. Also, if you find a particularly good way of saying something about an aspect of growth in one child that is true for another, you can clip and paste on a word processor and save some time.

- Always refer to your own classroom notes before you write these letters. This will improve the quality of your letters by making them more specific. Quoting your own notes in the letter is very powerful.

- Check to see what you said to parents in the last individualized letter before writing a new one. Try to build on your insights from letter to letter. For example, if you say in one letter that you hope to see a student take more risks using words whose spellings she is unsure of, give an update on that point in the next letter so that parents will know you have been working on and watching for this growth in their child's writing.

- Be specific about one or two areas of growth you have seen in the child's writing; spelling in use will obviously be a part of this. Cite examples so parents will know on what evidence you are judging this growth. You might photocopy a piece or two of the child's writing that demonstrate the growth, or quote the child directly if the growth was noticed in the child's actions rather than in his or her writing.

- Be specific about one or two areas where you want to help the child grow next as a writer. If possible, suggest how the parent can help the child grow as a writer in these areas.

- Keep the tone professional but approachable. Stay away from jargon.

- Invite parents to write back to you about what they see at home in their child's growth as a writer.

Sample Parent Letters

(*to the parents of Christina, discussed in Chapter 3*)

Dear Mr. and Mrs. Gomez,

Greetings! I am writing to update you on Christina's recent growth as a writer. Last Monday I sat and watched Christina write, and I noticed that she used primarily one strategy for getting her words down on paper—"sounding out." I confirmed this strategy for her. She wrote very fast by sounding out, showing that she has confidence in her knowledge of letters and sounds. To help her grow, I talked with Christina about using other strategies to get her words down on paper. I told her to think about what words look like from her reading (because some sounds you can't hear) and to think about whether the word was a long word or a short word. I also reminded her to make spaces between her words. Well, as you can see from the two examples, these new strategies already are taking hold in Christina's writing. Bravo! My next goal with Christina is to get her to use more variety in her writing—writing poems, letters, stories, etc. You might encourage her to do some of these at home. I'm excited about her growth.

Sincerely,

Mrs. Vargas

(*to the mother of Kelvin, discussed in Chapter 3*)

Dear Mrs. Almonte,

Hello from our busy classroom! Kelvin continues to love writing workshop (I saw him hug a piece of paper the other day), and I am very excited about his growth—we've had a breakthrough. For weeks I've been trying to understand what strategies he was using to get his words down for his writing. The other day I sat by him and just watched him write. I realized he was looking around the room and just writing down letters he saw (oh my!). His "words" had nothing to do with what he was thinking about his writing. I talked to Kelvin about this and helped him use the strategies I'd been teaching to the whole class (picturing what words look like, "sounding out," making long words long and short words short) that day. Since then, Kelvin literally has become a new writer (as you can see from these samples). He can read what's there and so can his classmates and I. For now I believe it is best for Kelvin to keep using these strategies and grow with them a while. But soon I want to work with him on staying with a story over time. He tends to start a new piece every day, even when there is a lot more to the ones he leaves behind. Anyway, I'm excited about this breakthrough—ask Kelvin to tell you about it.

Sincerely,

Ms. Watson

A Newsletter for Parents

Some teachers find it very effective to maintain ongoing lines of communication with parents through a regular newsletter. Your newsletter could consist of many typical items, reporting events and happenings in the classroom and school. However, you and your students also could use the newsletter as a vehicle for communicating how the writing curriculum encompasses instruction in spelling. In every issue you or a student could highlight a new spelling strategy, explaining how it is used and showing examples of how it has helped in students' writing during that news period. Using the "patterns and rules" focus used by Kevin (as described in Chapter 4), you might have a child share the word(s) under study for the week, as well as the patterns and insights gained through that study. You could also provide some writing samples to demonstrate how children in the classroom are making use of those new insights.

Your newsletter might also be a place to address concerns expressed by parents or those concerns you anticipate. You could utilize your own professional knowledge base and elaborate with information you have read in professional materials, such as books and journal articles (see bibliography). Outlined below is information we frequently share with parents to help them understand the knowledge base that informs our instruction, particularly in relation to the teaching of spelling in use. We have tried to preserve the tone of how this information is best shared with parents, and we encourage you to use as much of it as you see fit for newsletter type correspondence with parents. This particular piece would be useful when addressing parents' questions and concerns about constructed spelling.

Information About the Developmental Nature of Spelling

As my son learned to walk, we celebrated his first steps. When he toddled only a step or two before falling, we focused on the two steps. We gave him praise for his attempts, for his successful two steps. We encouraged him to stand up and try again. In short, he found himself in a supportive environment where the people he trusted most saw his attempts as progress toward independence.

As he learned to talk, we listened intently to his utterances. We focused on what he had to say, the message he wanted to send. When he said "kitty gone," we acknowledged his attempt to produce language and validated his successful communication. We responded, "Yes, the kitty is gone. The kitty went in the yard, but she'll come back." This sort of elaboration accomplishes several things at once:

- It repeats and validates the child's message.

- It models a standard form of language while communicating the same intent.

- It demonstrates that we value the child and what he or she has to say.

- It serves as a scaffold upon which the child can build and extend his or her own understanding of how language works.

As a child begins to write, the adults in his or her life need to be equally supportive and accepting of the child's early attempts with written language. Several aspects of a child's development merit mention:

- Handwriting may be "sprawling," lacking control over adultlike formation as a child slowly develops a more legible form.

- Early writing may be tied to drawings and occur as one-word labels or short phrases that communicate only a basic message about the drawing.

- Awareness of the sounds of letters will increase as a child attempts to invent or construct spellings to communicate thoughts.

- As a child writes, constructed spelling will progress toward an adult standard, much as the child's speech progressed from strings of sounds ("da-da") to complete sentences and elaborated speech.

- As with speech, the more demonstrations adults provide in natural contexts to show how written language works, the more a child will continue to explore and approximate those behaviors that will satisfy his or her need to communicate.

As children reach school age and begin writing for audiences beyond the home, it is their constructed spellings that tend to concern adults most. Many adults focus on the fact that children's constructed spellings are not correct when compared to standard dictionary spellings. Adults often perceive these constructed spellings (also called invented spellings or temporary spellings) as errors or mistakes that need to be corrected immediately before bad habits are learned. To the contrary, constructed spellings actually provide insight into children's understanding of letter-to-sound correspondences and spelling patterns. It is also through constructing spellings that children develop an awareness of the need for and benefits of standard spelling.

Remember that your goal in communicating with parents is to invite them to celebrate their child's learning with you. Your role is to help parents see the intelligence in the approximations children make as they take the necessary risks to gain experience with conventional spelling. Every language move a child makes comes from some evolving theory the child is using to make sense. Help parents suspend their adult logic (Laminack 1991) and see this theoretical brilliance in their children.

CHAPTER 6
Questions and Possibilities

Questions. We love questions. They keep us growing, keep us thinking. When we share our thinking with students and colleagues, spelling is one topic that never fails to generate many questions. Through many conversations about spelling questions, we have come to the conclusion that there are very few single answers or "quick-fix" solutions to most of the issues that perplex us. Instead of answers to questions, we need ways to make good decisions in our teaching with regard to spelling. Sometimes the "answers" that inform our decisions will be different. What we need are ways to think about our questions—points that help us consider our own beliefs and that structure our looking to children for the answers they may hold.

Below are six questions that have come up in one form or another in many of our conversations about the teaching of writing. In response, we offer points to consider that we believe will help you in your own classroom decision making.

Question One: When do you stop letting children use constructed spelling? Points to consider:

- First, let's look closely at the question. The word *letting* seems to convey the idea of "granting permission" to children to use constructed spelling. This is not an issue of permission, however; it is an issue of understanding. We don't *let* children construct spellings, as if they had some other options to say what they need to say; we understand that they *must* construct spellings if they are to do the work of writers.

- All writers construct spellings throughout their lives for words that are unfamiliar. The more experience writers have, the more strategies they develop and the fewer constructions are needed. This is always true. Constructing spellings is not a stage a writer outgrows, with conventional spelling being the end goal. It is something writers learn to handle throughout their lives.

- We always encourage children to write for audiences *using all the powerful things they know* about writing— including strategies for spelling, and we have high expectations for our students. If we feel a student is not using all her knowledge about writing, for example, we intervene and try to teach her past this. At the same time, we also understand that all writers will need to seek spelling assistance when writing for certain audiences. There is no time when this need is not present— not in our entire writing lives.

Question Two: What about word lists? Points to consider:

- Let's think about the general assumption behind word lists: that we learn to spell one word at a time—that there is a moment when we don't know how to spell a word, and then a later moment when we do. We do not believe that the conventional spellings we hold come to us in moments of time. We believe they come in layers of experiences with reading and writing. The "moment in time" learning may happen with a very few words that we own—words such as *Mississippi,* where the gim-

mick of the spelling was fixed in our minds the first time
we heard it—but this is a rare occasion.

- Spelling instruction can focus on spelling patterns and
  strategies, growing out of the context of the writer's
  work and questions.

- Some writers do, in fact, use a sort of listing strategy to
  help them remember tricky words that they use often.
  Our friend Barbara keeps a little note on her computer
  to help her remember the difference between the
  spelling of *chose* and *choose*. Our friend Jane keeps a reminder on her desk to help her with *familiar* and
  similar. "Those *i*'s and *a*'s can be so confusing!" she
  says. The significant point to remember here is that this
  is a very selective "list" initiated by the writer as a strategy for spelling troublesome words.

Question Three: Should I have my students keep personal
dictionaries of words they need help remembering? Points to
consider:

- One important thing to think about here is, "Whose purpose will this serve?" As teachers, we must ask ourselves if we want children to keep personal dictionaries
  because it's a good strategy for a writer, or because we
  hope to see fewer constructive spellings in children's
  writing.

- Another thing to consider is how we envision children
  using personal dictionaries. We need to articulate a vision of use for any structure that we put in place for all
  students in our classrooms. Once children begin to use
  a structure we've put in place, we must continuously reflect on its use to see if it matches what we envisioned.

- For writers to use dictionaries for spelling help in any
  productive way, they must own the spellings of most

words they need in their writing. A writer can't stop again and again to look up words. Many adult writers never interrupt their writing for this, choosing to deal with spelling issues after all their writing is complete. For us to expect young writers to look up words they don't know, in the same way adults would use this strategy, is unrealistic. There are just too many words for which young writers don't own the spellings. There is no way they could employ this strategy without it interfering with their meaning making.

- When teachers encourage children to use dictionaries for spelling help, they often see these children begin to limit themselves to using words that are in their dictionaries. Remember the example of Paola in Chapter 3.

Question Four: When children are writing and don't know how to spell a word, should I spell it for them if they ask? Points to consider:

- First, ask yourself, "Why is the child asking for a spelling?" The answer to this question always lies with the child. If eight-year-old Robert routinely and confidently constructs spellings for words he needs in his writing, his occasional asking for a spelling is a good strategy—one that many writers use. Robert has probably asked for the spelling because the word perplexes him in a way that most unfamiliar words do not. On the other hand, if Sara seems afraid to construct spellings for most unfamiliar words, she likely asks for spellings because she is reluctant to take risks or because she has a limited repertoire of strategies. She needs more work with strategies for constructing spellings for unfamiliar words.

- We must consider the possibility that when we routinely offer spellings to children we may be creating codependent relationships. Although feeling needed as teachers can be satisfying, it does little to make our students the independent writers we want them to be.

Question Five: Why do children spell words conventionally on a spelling test, and then misspell them in their writing? Points to consider:

- On spelling tests, the point of children's work is to get correct spellings for specific words. The focus of their attention is clearly on generating conventional spellings. In writing, the point of children's work is on making meaning, so the focus of their attention is understandably diverted away from spelling.

- A spelling test is essentially an act of simple memory and recall. Writing, on the other hand, is a much more complex act of continuous generation—generation of ideas, sentence structures, text features, and, of course, spellings.

- Related to this question is the difference between very young writers spending their writing time copying text versus spending time generating text. You may have observed what many wise teachers have: when encountering unknown spellings, the "generators" come up with much better spellings than the "copiers" because they've had so much more experience at what a writer must do when unknown spellings are encountered. Copying in no way replicates or gives children experience generating text. Preparation for spelling tests, likewise, gives writers no experience in generating text as needed.

Question Six: Should I give grades in spelling? Points to consider:

- The things we give grades for should reflect what is valued most in the classroom.

- On the other hand, a grade by itself, on anything, is an extremely narrow evaluative view of a child's learning and/or performance. The grade itself doesn't help the child's learning or the teacher's teaching. There just isn't enough information in a grade, and it represents merely a small part of the child's total literacy development.

- Sandra Wilde has noted that we feel compelled to give grades in spelling because it is a feature of writing that is very visible, even though it is not in any way the most important feature. She has said that giving separate grades in spelling and writing is like giving separate grades for multiplication and mathematics.

- If you as a teacher want a way to look evaluatively at children's spelling use, refer to Chapter 3 and look closely at the index of control. This index can give you a qualitative and quantitative picture of children's conventional spelling use. Although we realize that the numbers generated from the index could be converted to grades for spelling, we feel strongly that this should not happen. If children know that they are being graded for conventional spellings, they will begin to focus on this at the expense of meaning making, and it is likely that they will take fewer risks as writers.

Question Seven: What about spelling books? Should I use the exercises as extra resources for my writers? Points to consider:

- The exercises in spelling books are made-up work where there is no work to be done. This is why the exercises often seem so senseless and, when they are assigned as homework, require whole families to figure out what's to be done. There just isn't any work to be done on "practicing" with spelling. There are not any layers to understanding spellings. You don't deepen your knowledge of how to spell a word, so any attempts to make the study of individual words into meaningful study are purposeless.

CONCLUSION

We learn through reflection. E. M. Forster has been quoted as saying, "I never know what I think until I see what I say." In a very real sense, the writing of this book has helped us to see what we say and know better what we think. Our own words have become a text for our reflection, and we have learned from them. Over and over we have noticed certain themes behind our words, sometimes appearing very clearly in a story or an insight, other times living underneath the ideas—harder to see, but just as important to our thinking.

Now that we see what we say behind our words and underneath our ideas, we have discovered that we think:

- All writers are spellers, but not all spellers are writers.

- Writers need tools (spelling, genre structures, punctuation, etc.) to write with power. The tools by themselves, though, are not important. Powerful writing is important.

- For spelling instruction to make sense, it needs to happen alongside the real work of writers. This is the only way teachers can know what a child can do and what that child needs to know.

- The best teaching about language happens when children are invited, through predictable structures, to be curious researchers of how language works.

- Teachers must know curriculum well enough (apart from manuals and textbooks) to meet students "head-on" in their work. Distant authors of manuals can never know the students we teach and so cannot do this "head-on" teaching.

- We have come to believe that *constructed spelling* is the most appropriate term for the spellings that writers generate because this term reflects the constructive nature of learning.

We learn through questions. As we reread this text, as much as we are confirmed to see what we think, we are left with lingering questions. The more we know, as they say, the more we see we need to know. We have made peace with this in our teaching, embracing anomalies because we trust them to keep us learning. We love what Parker Palmer (1990) has said: "Truth is an eternal conversation about things that matter, conducted with passion and discipline." Our questions keep us in the eternal conversation:

- What kinds of classroom questions and research do we need to help further our understandings about how writers come to control language use?

- To what extent will technology (spell-check, Internet, e-mail) impact this conversation about spelling and its role in a writer's life?

- To what extent will politics continue to impact this conversation, and, with regard to the empowerment of a generation of writers, how political must we be in defending our stance?

- What are the best ways to reeducate a professional work force of teachers schooled from a more traditional paradigm of language learning, and do we have the right to assume that this reeducation should take place?

- What kinds of implicit knowledge do writers hold that help them own the spellings of many words? Can we make this kind of knowledge more explicit?

- What kind of writers would we have if children were consistently exposed throughout their school years to instruction in writing that valued spelling in use, instead of accumulating years of mixed messages in hit-and-miss instruction? In other words, what's possible? What new insights could be gained from studying these writers?

We learn through stories. Our lives in classrooms are filled with a hundred small narratives a day, each with its own beginning, middle, and end—or sometimes, "to be continued." This book has been filled with the lessons we have learned from being students of our teaching stories, so it is only fitting that we should end with one more story—a personal story, one more window into our *current understanding* about the role of spelling instruction in our teaching of writing.

It is spring. Katie is on a committee at the university to select an outstanding faculty member for excellence in teaching, and she is reading through a stack of nomination forms from students. On one of these forms the first line reads, "Dr. Rose is very eger [sic] to help her students." Katie is floored by this, and a few moments later when she realizes she is floored by the misspelling, she is again floored at her own reaction to it. Isn't she the "writing woman" who repeatedly tries to help her students understand how much more important the message is than the way it's spelled? How could she be offended at a college student's misspelling of a word in the first line of a nomination form?

Together, we thought through this story, looking for some new understanding we were certain lay in its dénouement. Essentially, we realized that the understanding to this story lay

in the answer to one question. If this college student had been
a student in our, say, fourth-grade classroom, would we have
put in a better day teaching if we had made her write *eager*
fifty more times until she "got it," or if we had spent our energy
on turning her into *the kind of writer* who knew to get someone
to proofread her writing for certain, high-stakes audiences
(such as a nomination committee)?

Our answer to this question was, of course, we would have
spent more time teaching toward the kind of writer we hoped
she would become, not more time focused on a certain word.
Clearly, it was unacceptable for a college student to "go public
with" (publish) a piece of writing to a distant audience (the
nomination committee) with a misspelling in it. We know it is
not important that the college student (or any writer) hold
onto the spelling of all the words she might ever want to use.
What is important is that she assess her audience and know
how to prepare her writing accordingly—including checking
spelling when her writing will lose power if there are mis-
spellings in it.

In the end, what we have to understand about writing curriculum, particularly with regard to spelling, is that we can
never anticipate all the specific things our writers will need to
know at specific times in their lives. It would be presumptuous
of us to think we could. We must nurture, instead, a "curriculum of being" (Wood 1995) that initiates writers into a way of
being as writers—writers who care deeply about what they
have to say and can get those messages prepared with power
to go out and rock the world. Young writers need all the curriculum help we can give them to write with power, but we as
teachers must remember that the "stuff" of the curriculum—
like the conventional spelling of *eager*—is never the point. The
child and the life he or she now lives and will someday live as
a writer is the point.

Does this sound like just semantics? We believe that understanding and taking this curricular stance of being is a whole
paradigm away from a stance where the stuff of curriculum,

particularly the isolated focus on spelling words, seems to be the whole point of instruction. We hope *Spelling in Use* will help open conversations and encourage new thinking about looking at children as writers who have many tools at their disposal, including spelling, to write with power in the world. One child's life as a writer is the point.

WORKS CITED

Bouffler, Christine. 1984. Spelling as a language process. In *Reading, writing, and spelling* (Proceedings of the fifth Macarthur reading/language symposium, Sydney, ed. L. Unsworth). Quoted in Brian Cambourne and Jan Turbill, *Coping with chaos* (Portsmouth, New Hampshire: Heinemann, 1991), 24–25.

Calkins, Lucy McCormick. 1994. *The art of teaching writing: new edition.* Portsmouth, New Hampshire: Heinemann.

Cambourne, Brian. 1988. *The whole story: Natural learning and the acquisition of literacy in the classroom.* New York: Scholastic.

Cambourne, Brian, and Jan Turbill. 1991. *Coping with chaos.* Portsmouth, New Hampshire: Heinemann.

Cochrane, Orin, Donna Cochrane, Sharm Scalena, and Ethel Buchanan. 1984. *Reading, writing, and caring.* Katonah, New York: Richard C. Owen Publishers.

Dakos, Kalli. 1993. *Don't read this book, whatever you do!* New York: Macmillan Publishing Company.

Fletcher, Ralph. 1993. *What a writer needs.* Portsmouth, New Hampshire: Heinemann.

Goodman, Ken. 1986. *What's whole in whole language.* Portsmouth, New Hampshire: Heinemann.

Graves, Donald. 1983. *Writing: Teachers and children at work.* Portsmouth, New Hampshire: Heinemann.

Halliday, Michael A. K. 1973. *Explorations in the functions of language.* London: Edward Arnold.

Laminack, Lester. 1991. *Learning with Zachary.* Richmond Hill, Ontario: Scholastic-TAB.

North Carolina Department of Public Instruction. 1989. *Grades 1 and 2 Assessment: Communication Skills.* Raleigh.

Palmer, Parker. 1990. Good teaching: A matter of living the mystery. *Change* Jan/Feb:12.

Smith, Frank. 1978. *Reading without nonsense.* New York: Teachers College Press.

———. 1988. *Joining the literacy club: Further essays into education.* Portsmouth, New Hampshire: Heinemann.

Wilde, Sandra. 1989. Looking at invented spelling: A kid-watcher's guide to spelling, part 1. In *The whole language evaluation book,* ed. Kenneth Goodman, Yetta Goodman, and Wendy Hood, 213–26. Portsmouth, New Hampshire: Heinemann.

———. 1989. Understanding spelling strategies: A kidwatcher's guide to spelling, part 2. In *The whole language evaluation book,* ed. Kenneth Goodman, Yetta Goodman, and Wendy Hood, 227–36. Portsmouth, New Hampshire: Heinemann.

———. 1992. *You kan red this! Spelling and punctuation for whole language classrooms, K–6.* Portsmouth, New Hampshire: Heinemann.

Wood, Katie. 1995. "Developing a curriculum of being." Keynote address given at the Summer Institute of The Writing Project, Teachers College, Columbia University, New York.

AFTERWORD

It was a surprise for me to learn that Katie Wood and Lester Laminack had written a book on spelling! I know them both as *writing* people. I picture Katie, standing at the podium of the Teachers College Writing Project Institute, with throngs of admiring teachers all around her. She is talking about the craft of writing, regaling us with stories of children who write with grace and wingspan and intention. I can feel again the fullness of the silence when she closes Cynthia Rylant's *Missing May,* and we'll sit in quiet reverence, letting the wake of this story wash over us. "A book on spelling?" I asked.

But then I saw the book, and I understand. The power of this small gem of a book is that it is a book about spelling written by two people who love reading and writing, story and memoir, song and poetry. It's a book about spelling by two people who know that spelling is for writing, that spelling is meant as a tool for reaching wide audiences, that it's meant to have a place—but only a place—in the wholeness of our curriculum. How precious it is to have a book that efficiently gathers together the field's wisdom on spelling, highlighting some particularly useful insights. How useful it is to have a book that suggests a handful of effective, small, easily-managed strategies for supporting our children as spellers.

But the book's biggest contribution is that Katie and Lester build on that base of knowledge, and share with us their own insights about spelling. These insights grow from people who understand well—who helped to invent—the central tenets used by those who teach and write about the writing workshop.

I know of few professionals who know more about conferring with students around rough draft writing; now Katie and Lester take that wisdom and incorporate it into strategies for the teaching of spelling. I know of few professionals who are wiser about ways to support teachers as they grow. Now Katie and Lester take that wisdom, too, and incorporate it into their thinking about the development in the area of spelling.

—Lucy Calkins

INDEX

Lester Laminack is chair of the Department of Elementary and Middle Grades Education at Western Carolina University, Cullowhee, North Carolina. He teaches graduate and undergraduate literacy classes, is a past member of the Whole Language Umbrella Board of Directors, is a current member of the board of the Center for Expansion of Language and Thinking, and is actively involved in state and national literacy organizations. He is an author, a teacher, and most of all a learner.

Katie Wood is an assistant professor in the Department of Elementary and Middle Grades Education at Western Carolina University, where she teaches graduate and undergraduate courses in language arts and children's literature. She is also a consultant in the New York Public Schools with the Writing Project, Teachers College, Columbia University.